W9-DDB-960

# PURE MICHIGAN®

## Eating Fresh and Local in the Great Lakes State

PHOTOGRAPH: KEVIN J. MIYAZAKI/REDUX

# PURE *M*ICHIGAN®

## Eating Fresh and Local in the Great Lakes State

BY THE EDITORS OF *MIDWEST LIVING*® MAGAZINE

MEREDITH CORPORATION | DETROIT

Copyright 2011 © Meredith Corporation

All rights reserved. No part of this book may be reproduced or transmitted in any form without written permission from the publisher: Meredith Corporation, 1716 Locust St., Des Moines, Iowa 50309.

Meredith Corporation: Detroit, Chicago, New York, Des Moines, Iowa

ISBN 978-0-696-30060-8

Library of Congress Cataloging-in-Publication Data is available.

Printed in Ann Arbor, Michigan
First Edition/First Printing

Photographs *(From left)*: Kevin J. Miyazaki/Redux, Robert Jacobs, Jason Lindsey, Kritsada.
Front cover *(Clockwise from top)*: Per Breiehagen, Kevin J. Miyazaki/ Redux (3).
Back cover: Bob Stefko. Inside flaps *(Front to back)*: Kevin J. Miyazaki/Redux,
Robert Jacobs

## PURE
# Innovation

## PURE
# Inspiration

## PURE
# Tradition

PHOTOGRAPHS: KEVIN J. MIYAZAKI/REDUX

# PURE MICHIGAN

One of the best ways to experience a place is to taste it—literally. During almost 25 years of traveling the Midwest, we've found few spots where those tastes are more soul-satisfying than in Michigan. Experiences and local flavors mingle and enrich each other in especially memorable ways along 3,000-plus miles of shore, across vast waterfall-laced wilderness and in comeback cities. Imagine walking on a golden beach and then savoring a meal along a postcard-pretty Main Street just steps from the sand. You share a chef's creations and glasses of local wine in a bistro tucked among galleries, pretty shops and other eateries. Artisan-made bread and cheeses complete the feast. Afterward, you stroll, deciding between handcrafted chocolates and pie filled with Michigan cherries. Where's this town? Dozens of Michigan spots fit that description. Actually, there seem to be food artisans, chefs and committed cooks at work almost everywhere in the state. They and all the Michigan places we love inspired this book. We hope you use it to experience Pure Michigan and re-create those tastes at home.

A quail's egg caps the sushi-grade ahi tuna at Detroit's Saltwater. For recipe, see page 144. *(Opposite)* Chef Craig Common crafts inspired bistro fare at The Common Grill in Chelsea.

PHOTOGRAPHS: KEVIN J. MIYAZAKI/REDUX

# {PURE}
# Innovation

Michigan's vibrant food scene gets richer by the day as an innovative generation of chefs joins established masters. Blending talent and passion, these chefs are reinventing menus with an emphasis on the bounty of the state's lakes, orchards and farms. Detroit, Grand Rapids and Traverse City all host rich and increasingly diverse culinary scenes. But don't overlook smaller Michigan towns, where inspired dining also flourishes.

*(From left)* Once a rail ticket station, now Grand Trunk Pub. A tantilizing dessert from Detroit's Rattlesnake Club.

# Exploring the Motor City

THERE'S NEVER BEEN a better time to savor the ever-changing flavors of Detroit as Motown embraces a new generation of inspired chefs and downtown restaurants.

A few blocks northeast of downtown's business towers, the celebrated Rattlesnake Club serves a sophisticated menu with an accent on Michigan grown and produced ingredients. Chef Jimmy Schmidt received the James Beard Award for culinary excellence.

At Bourbon Steak in the posh MGM Grand Detroit Casino and Resort, chef Michael Mina is redefining the contemporary steak house in both menu and ambience.

Chef Matt Prentice oversees several metro restaurants. He's best known for the innovative contemporary American menu and extensive wine list at his swank Coach Insignia. The restaurant commands panoramic views of Detroit and neighboring Canada from its perch on the glass-walled 71st floor of the GM Global Renaissance Center. Another advocate of local ingredients, Matt even founded Sourdough Bread Factory in Pontiac to supply his restaurants with artisan loaves and pastries.

## TASTES GUIDE

Detroit's esteemed new chefs and restaurants enhance an already incredibly diverse culinary scene in this cultural melting pot. Detroit was built into an automotive powerhouse over the course of a century by workers migrating from the fields and forests of America and the farms and cities of the Old World. They built Greektown, opened Polish groceries, brought recipes for sweet potato pie, grew the vegetables, and raised the beef, poultry and lamb that now make the city's vast Eastern Market a wonder of agricultural bounty. Along the way, the immigrants introduced Motown to a world of flavors. For more information, links and ideas, visit michigan.org.

**AL-AMEER** Detroit boasts the nation's largest population of Arab Americans. Al-Ameer serves award-winning Middle Eastern and Lebanese cuisine at two Dearborn locations.

**BAKER'S KEYBOARD LOUNGE** At the jazz club billed as the world's oldest, music is served with sides of black-eyed peas, collard greens and coleslaw.

**BEANS & CORNBREAD** Soul food favorites ranging from fried chicken to salmon croquettes and sweet potato muffins make this casually elegant

PHOTOGRAPHS: KEVIN J. MIYAZAKI/REDUX

*(From left)* Relaxing on the Detroit riverfront. The People Mover, a light-rail shuttle.

Detroit's esteemed new chefs and restaurants enhance an already incredibly diverse culinary scene of global flavors in this cultural melting pot.

restaurant a favorite in a city with a rich African American heritage.

**BUDDY'S PIZZERIA** This small local chain gets credit for serving the first Detroit-style pizza in 1946; it's a square, deep-dish pie with the sauce on top.

**EASTERN MARKET** Come Saturday and come hungry to buy just-picked vegetables, baked goods, bedding plants, meats, and other regional ingredients and food items on sale by more than 250 independent vendors.

**FISHBONE'S RHYTHM KITCHEN CAFE** New Orleans' French Quarter comes to Greektown in this kingdom of gumbos, grits and live music.

**GOOD GIRLS GO TO PARIS CREPES** Fortunately, some of the girls stay home in Midtown Detroit to prepare 50 varieties of savory crepes with fillings ranging from Nutella to lox.

**GRAND TRUNK PUB** Once the ticket office of the Grand Trunk Railroad, this ornate downtown space now is a shrine to Michigan craft beers and a worthwhile stop for shepherd's pie and eggs and hash.

**MR. PAUL'S CHOP HOUSE** Founded in 1968, this Roseville institution is almost as famous for its friendly ambience as it is for the 22-ounce USDA prime porterhouse.

**PEGASUS TAVERNA** In Greektown, with a second restaurant in St. Clair Shores, sip a glass of retsina wine with your *saganaki*, moussaka and kabob.

**POLISH MARKET** Come for the kielbasa and grandma's ham at the meat counter; stay for the pierogi and cabbage rolls in the deli at stores in Troy, Hamtramck and Macomb.

**THE WHITNEY** Dinner and drinks are served nightly in elegant splendor at this pink-stone 1894 mansion that became a restaurant in 1986.

## BETWEEN MEALS

**CASINOS** Gaming and a swank hotel and restaurants are hallmarks of the Greektown Casino-Hotel, where you can dine at acclaimed Bistro 555; MotorCity Casino-Hotel, home of Iridescence Restaurant; and the MGM Grand Detroit, which houses Bourbon Steak and Saltwater restaurants.

PHOTOGRAPHS: KEVIN J. MIYAZAKI/REDUX

**CHARLES H. WRIGHT MUSEUM OF AFRICAN AMERICAN HISTORY** Detroit is home to the world's largest institution honoring the African-American experience.

**COMERICA PARK** The Tigers play here, but the downtown ballpark also tempts with a Ferris wheel, carousel, batting cages and other amusements.

**CONEYS** More than 30 restaurants serve the hometown favorite: hotdogs smothered in meat sauce. Downtown, neighboring American Coney Island and Lafayette Coney Island claim legendary loyalty from their customers.

**CRANBROOK** The 319-acre National Historic Landmark includes a 1908 Arts and Crafts mansion, museums and 40 acres of gardens.

**DETROIT INSTITUTE OF ARTS** In addition to Diego Rivera's famous *Detroit Industry* frescos, the recently renovated museum is a browser's delight with 100 galleries of American and international art.

**FOX THEATRE** The word *opulent* hardly does justice to this 1928 movie palace, the nation's second-largest theater, now hosting Broadway plays, rock concerts, symphonies and more.

**GUARDIAN BUILDING** It's worth taking a peek into the cathedrallike lobby of this circa 1929 jewel box of an office tower in the Financial District.

**MOTOWN MUSEUM** In these humble connected houses on Grand Avenue, Marvin Gaye, Stevie Wonder, The Supremes and other artists made the music that defined a generation.

**PEWABIC POTTERY** Since 1903, Pewabic has crafted distinctive Arts and Crafts-style tiles, vases and other creations featuring iridescent glazes.

**RENAISSANCE CENTER** Anchoring downtown, the iconic seven-tower complex is home to a posh Marriott and GMs' world headquarters.

**WILLIAM G. MILLIKEN STATE PARK AND HARBOR** Dedicated in 2009, Michigan's first urban state park stands along the Detroit River.

## FIVE FABULOUS PLATES

### Apps@Coach Insignia
The glass-walled central tower of the **Ren Cen** houses this rooftop restaurant. Comfortable bites, such as grilled lamb loin and chilled poached shrimp, share the menu with go-ahead-try-it specialties: lobster corn dogs and smoked salmon tostadas.

### Veggies@Rattlesnake
Michigan's bounty stars in a creamy sweet pea and fennel risotto, the juicy heirloom tomato Napoleon, and a salad of golden and ruby beets at this riverfront restaurant.

### Beef@Bourbon Steak
One of MGM Grand Detroit's signature restaurants, Bourbon Steak specializes in high-quality beef dishes. Among the specialties of the house: prime cuts gently poached in butter and then nudged to tender perfection on a wood-fired grill.

### Seafood@Saltwater
The choices are delectably varied, from ahi tuna poppers and gulf shrimp fritters to coconut shrimp bisque and miso-glazed sea scallops, at this signature MGM Grand Detroit restaurant.

### Sweets@Roma Cafe
Since 1890, tuxedo-clad waiters at Detroit's oldest Italian restaurant have served traditional classics. For dessert, try the crisp cannoli, plump with sweetened ricotta and chocolate. Or the lush rum, pistachio and chocolate spumoni. One of each?

Downtown Detroit rises above its namesake river. (*Opposite*) Dubbed the Cathedral of Finance, the ornate 1929 Guardian Building anchors the Detroit Financial District.

# DARK-SPICE-TUMBLED BEEF TENDERLOIN

*Chefs are always coming up with new spins on techniques. At the Rattlesnake Club, chef Jimmy Schmidt uses a vacuum tumbling machine to enhance meat with aromatic spices. He adapted the recipe so at-home cooks could make it.*

Prep: 1½ hours  Grill: 18 minutes  Stand: 10 minutes

- 1 750-milliliter bottle full-bodied dry red wine, such as Cabernet Sauvignon or Syrah
- 2 tablespoons honey
- 3 tablespoons unsweetened cocoa powder
- 2 tablespoons instant espresso coffee powder
- 1 tablespoon sea salt or 1½ teaspoons salt
- 1 tablespoon ground New Mexico chile pepper or chili powder
- 1 tablespoon freshly ground black Tellicherry peppercorns or ground black pepper
- 16 fresh asparagus spears
- 2 teaspoons Carotino red palm fruit oil or olive oil

- Sea salt or salt
- Freshly ground black Tellicherry peppercorns or ground black pepper
- 4 6- to 8-ounce Certified Angus Beef tenderloin steaks, cut 1½ inches thick
- 1 tablespoon Carotino red palm fruit oil or olive oil
- Onion Tarts (see recipe, page 147)
- Potato Crisps (see recipe, page 147) (optional)
- 4 fresh rosemary sprigs (optional)
- 2 tablespoons rosemary-flavor olive oil (optional)

**1.** For wine sauce: In a large saucepan, stir together wine and honey. Bring to boiling; reduce heat. Boil gently, uncovered, about 35 minutes or until reduced to ½ cup and thickened enough to coat the back of a metal spoon. Transfer half of the sauce to a small bowl; set both portions aside.
**2.** For spice blend: In a shallow bowl or pie plate, stir together cocoa powder, espresso coffee powder, the 1 tablespoon sea salt, the ground chile pepper and the 1 tablespoon black pepper; set aside.
**3.** For asparagus: Snap off stem ends of asparagus. Rinse asparagus; drain. In a large nonstick skillet, heat the

2 teaspoons palm fruit oil over medium-high heat. Add asparagus. Cook, uncovered, for 3 to 5 minutes or until crisp-tender, stirring occasionally. Remove from heat; keep warm.
**4.** Rub both sides of steaks with the 1 tablespoon palm fruit oil. For charcoal grill: Place steaks on the rack of an uncovered grill directly over medium coals. Grill 15 to 19 minutes for medium-rare (145°) or 18 to 23 minutes for medium (160°), turning once halfway through grilling. (For gas grill: Preheat grill. Reduce heat to medium. Place steaks on grill rack over heat. Cover; grill as above.)
**5.** Remove steaks from grill; brush

both sides with one portion of the reserved wine sauce. Dip steaks into spice blend, turning to coat all sides. Return steaks to grill. Grill about 3 minutes more or until spice coating is lightly browned, turning once halfway through grilling. Transfer steaks to a large platter. Loosely cover steaks; let stand for 10 minutes before serving.
**6.** For each serving, place an Onion Tart on a plate. Top with a steak; drizzle steak with some of the remaining wine sauce. Serve with four asparagus spears. If you like, garnish with a Potato Crisp and rosemary; garnish plate with rosemary-flavor oil and remaining wine sauce. **Makes 4 servings.**

PHOTOGRAPHS: KEVIN J. MIYAZAKI/REDUX

# BUTTER-POACHED PORTERHOUSE

*Steaks grilled over coals and smothered in butter ooze good taste. At the restaurant, steaks poach in pans of butter then cook on a wood-burning grill. Now you can make this version of MGM Grand Detroit's Bourbon Steak signature dish at home.*

Prep: 30 minutes  Cook: 15 minutes  Grill: 10 minutes  Stand: 10 minutes

1  30-ounce beef porterhouse steak, cut about 1¼ inches thick
½  teaspoon kosher salt or ¼ teaspoon salt
¼  teaspoon freshly ground black pepper
   Bourbon Steak's Butter Sauce (recipe follows)
   Kosher salt or salt
   Freshly ground black pepper
   Roasted Garlic (see recipe, page 146)
2  or 3 baby sweet peppers (optional)
1  fresh tarragon or thyme sprig (optional)

**1.** Sprinkle steak with the ½ teaspoon kosher salt and the ¼ teaspoon black pepper. Place steak in a large saucepan with Bourbon Steak's Butter Sauce, making sure sauce covers the steak.
**2.** Cook over very low heat (120°) for 15 minutes, adjusting heat as needed to maintain 120°. (A grill probe placed under steak in saucepan or an instant-read thermometer works well to keep steak at proper temperature.) Remove steak from sauce; drain on a wire rack. Sprinkle with additional salt and black pepper. Discard sauce or use immediately to cook another steak.
**3.** For charcoal grill: Place steak on the rack of an uncovered grill directly over medium-hot coals. Grill 10 to 13 minutes for medium-rare (145°) or 12 to 16 minutes for medium (160°),

turning once halfway through grilling. (If flare-ups occur, temporarily move the steak to a cooler area of the grill.) (For gas grill: Preheat grill. Reduce heat to medium-high. Place steak on grill rack over heat. Cover; grill as directed.) Remove steak from grill. Place on a platter. Loosely cover steak; let stand for 10 minutes before serving.
**4.** Serve with Roasted Garlic. If you like, garnish with sweet peppers and tarragon. **Makes 2 or 3 servings.**
**Bourbon Steak's Butter Sauce:** Heat 2½ cups (five sticks) unsalted butter, without stirring, over very low heat until melted; cool slightly. Pour the clear top layer (clarified butter) into a large saucepan; discard the milky bottom layer. Add two shallots, sliced, and one fresh thyme sprig. **Makes 2 cups.**

## Steak house reinvented

Forget your assumptions about traditional steak houses. Located in the palatial new downtown MGM Grand Detroit, Bourbon Steak combines a striking blend of contemporary glass walls and mood lighting with weathered bricks and massive oak beams salvaged from local industrial buildings.

Chef Michael Mina's menu plays off that theme by putting a twist on classics. Steaks star with cuts of flavorful Piedmonte and Kobe beef poached in butter to melt-in-your-mouth tenderness then seared on a wood-fired grill visible behind one glass wall.

Served for two, a whole fried organic chicken comes with a side of truffled mac and cheese. Tradition is honored on the drink menu featuring old-fashioneds, Manhattans and other faithfully mixed classics. Diners also choose from a 34-plus-page wine menu.

PHOTOGRAPHS: KEVIN J. MIYAZAKI/REDUX

The colossal lump crab cake is a Rattlesnake Club seasonal favorite. (*Below, from left*) Painted on the walls of the Detroit Institute of Arts, Diego Rivera's 27 *Detroit Industry* frescos have captivated viewers since 1933. Detroit's Eastern Market has provided produce, meats and other ingredients to generations of chefs and home cooks.

# COLOSSAL CRAB CAKES WITH SALSA

*Rattlesnake Club's chef Jimmy Schmidt says, "This entree is a seasonal favorite. After a summer of feasting in the ocean and under the sun, both crab and tomatoes are plump and juicy." He serves his signature dish with two tantalizing salsas.*

Prep: 1 hour  Chill: 45 minutes  Bake: 15 minutes

|   |   |
|---|---|
| 1 | pound fresh or frozen lump crabmeat |
| ½ | cup finely chopped sweet onion |
| ¼ | cup finely chopped celery |
| ¼ | cup mayonnaise |
| ½ | teaspoon sea salt or ¼ teaspoon salt |
| ¼ | teaspoon cayenne pepper |
| ½ | cup finely crushed wheat crackers |
| 2 | tablespoons lime juice |
| 2 | tablespoons Citron vodka or vodka |
| 1½ | teaspoons Worcestershire sauce |
| 1 | teaspoon garlic salt |
| ¼ | teaspoon sea salt or ⅛ teaspoon salt |
| 1 | cup chopped yellow and/or orange heirloom or other tomato |
| 1½ | teaspoons cream-style prepared horseradish |
| ½ | cup chopped red heirloom or other tomato |
|   | Dash bottled hot chipotle pepper sauce |
|   | Fresh salad greens |
| 6 | small heirloom tomatoes or cherry tomatoes, halved |

**1.** For crab cakes: Thaw crabmeat, if frozen. Line a baking sheet with parchment paper; set aside. In a medium bowl, combine onion, celery, mayonnaise, the ½ teaspoon salt and the cayenne. Fold in crabmeat. Form crab mixture into four mounded cakes about 1½ inches tall and 2½ inches wide. Sprinkle half of the crushed crackers into four small circles on prepared baking sheet. Place a crab cake on each circle of crumbs. Lightly sprinkle tops of crab cakes with remaining crushed crackers. Cover and chill in freezer about 45 minutes or until cold (do not allow to freeze).

**2.** Meanwhile, combine lime juice, vodka, Worcestershire sauce, garlic salt and ¼ teaspoon salt. Set aside. *Continued on page 145*

## Fresh classic

Chef Jimmy Schmidt's renowned Rattlesnake Club (*above*) occupies a converted warehouse that claims most of a block on a tree-shaded cobblestone street with views of the Detroit River and RiverWalk. It also holds a special place in the Great Lakes State's burgeoning field-to-fork movement.

The club has built a reputation using locally grown and farm-raised ingredients— plump, ripe peaches, juicy heirloom tomatoes and lamb fattened by grazing on the tendrils of harvested peas.

"Michigan is a Green Giant state," Jimmy explains. "It only made sense."

Rattlesnake Club patrons settle into a contemporary dining room filled with magnificent pieces of abstract art. On balmy days, many dine on the covered patio, sharing space with urns of booming tomatoes and fragrant herbs— reminders of Jimmy's devotion to fresh and flavorful.

PHOTOGRAPHS: KEVIN J. MIYAZAKI/REDUX

In the JW Marriott, six.one.six restaurant serves an innovative contemporary menu. *(Right)* Roasted medallions of Kurobuta pork tenderloin at the Amway Grand Plaza.

## Another Grand Michigan City Scene

IN ADDITION TO a burgeoning art presence, the state's second-largest city boasts a top culinary school, more than 60 downtown restaurants, a cadre of leading chefs and a local-food scene that rivals any in the state or the region.

Graduates of the Secchia Institute for Culinary Education staff many kitchens. And a number of chefs rely on ingredients from the city's Fulton Street Farmers Market and area farms.

The restaurants at the heralded Four-Diamond Amway Grand Plaza, including a classic steak house opening this fall and cutting edge Cygnus 27, suggest the range of Grand Rapids fine dining. In the regal early-20th-century wing of the hotel, the steak house will serve dishes prepared by chef Christian Madsen. A South Haven native with a flair for

PHOTOGRAPHS: KEVIN J. MIYAZAKI/REDUX

French cuisine, the chef works easily with ingredients ranging from foie gras to Michigan spring beets.

Atop the neighboring 27-floor glass tower of the hotel's modern wing, the AAA Four-Diamond Cygnus 27 offers sweeping panoramas. Austrian-born chef Werner Absenger presents a global mix of flavors, such as five-spice braised pork belly and *chimichurri* swordfish.

Both chefs are devoted to using local ingredients. Chef Absenger even helps with a program encouraging cultivation of specialty produce for area restaurants on vacant city lots.

For pure devotion to locally grown, it's hard to top swank six.one.six in the JW Marriott, where chefs Joel Wabeke and Lindsey Vandentoorn help oversee the restaurant's garden.

## TASTES GUIDE

With a metro area of a million residents, Grand Rapids feels hip and cosmopolitan with its big-city amenities—first-rate museums, world-class sculptures and farm-to-table restaurants. The city also offers small-town perks such as affordable dining and lodging, plus walking trails along the banks of the Grand River.

**AMWAY GRAND PLAZA** Overlooking the Grand River, downtown's anchor, the überfriendly Amway is home to Cygnus 27 and four more restaurants, plus a spa and shopping plaza.

**BREAKFAST** Real Food Cafe is a local favorite for omelets, light and fluffy pancakes and, well, just about anything associated with the day's most important meal. Ditto Wolfgang's, home of English muffin toast, grilled cinnamon rolls and all things hollandaise.

**CHERRY DELI** Choose from more than 50 sandwiches—meat and veggie, hot and cold—all named after Grand Rapids streets and landmarks, then pair your choice with a crisp salad or from-scratch soup.

PHOTOGRAPH: JOHN NOLTNER

Downtown and the Grand Rapids Public Museum overlook the Grand River.

### FIVE FABULOUS PLATES

**Small Plates@Cygnus 27**
High atop the Amway Grand Plaza, inspired choices range from duck rangoon to melted raclette served with a crisp bagel and mussels in a red chili-pesto broth.

**Risotto@Tre Cugini**
Cooked-to-order risotto and made-fresh-daily gnocchi star at this authentic Italian restaurant. House specialties include veal and a wide selection of fresh fish. Dinner specials change weekly.

**Tapas@San Chez Bistro**
The well-packed menu of bites tempts with skewers of lamb loin and onion, ahi tuna ceviche and blue cheese fritters with red pepper aioli. Or feast on paella at this Fulton Street restaurant.

**Vino@Reserve**
In a hip, artistic setting, pair small plates big enough for sharing with one of more than 100 wines by the glass. We love the spinach and poached egg risotto.

**Drinks@six.one.six**
Located off the lobby of the JW Marriott, six.one.six challenges its bartenders to create one-of-a-kind beverages. Try the Dragon Martini made of pomegranate vodka, Pama liqueur and pickled ginger juice with sides of smoked pecans and cheesy pesto flatbread.

Michigan-built, the only surviving Driggs Skylark Biplane soars in the Grand Rapids Public Museum.

**FULTON STREET FARMERS MARKET** Since 1922, the market has offered fresh fruits and veggies, meat, and eggs as well as arts and crafts.

**GAIA CAFE** This casual East Hills neighborhood restaurant serves inventive vegetarian and vegan dishes. Daily there's a brown rice risotto special at lunch, or fill up on a hearty breakfast dish like the Jim White.

**HILL BROS. ORCHARDS** Family owned since 1843, this you-pick orchard is as popular as its legendary cider.

**MARIE CATRIB'S** Middle Eastern flavors star on this eclectic from-scratch menu that includes vegan soups and lasagna.

**YESTERDOG** The hotdog eatery's decor is 1930s hip, and customers toss tips into an old gramophone horn.

## BETWEEN MEALS

**GERALD R. FORD MUSEUM** Overlooking the Grand River, the museum honors the city's famous native son with holographic displays, interactive video and hands-on exhibits. A 1970s gallery features a Watergate exhibit.

**GRAND RAPIDS ART MUSEUM** A century old in 2010 and beautifully renovated to be the first LEED-certified museum in the world, GRAM displays an extensive collection of paintings, sculpture and other art. Saturday is family day, with opportunities for parents and children to learn about and create art together.

**GRAND RAPIDS CHILDREN'S MUSEUM** Schedule a play day for the kids at the downtown museum dedicated to showing children how to enjoy and create art. The museum hosts many special events and seasonal exhibits.

**GRAND RAPIDS PUBLIC MUSEUM** Step into re-created street scenes of Grand Rapids in the 1890s and peruse permanent and visiting exhibits.

**JOHN BALL ZOO** Visitors get close to more than 1,100 animals from all over the world, including Michigan's only Komodo dragon.

**JW MARRIOTT** The downtown luxury hotel features the renowned six.one.six restaurant and a spa.

**MILLENNIUM PARK** Twice the size of New York City's Central Park, this 1,500-acre enclave is a mosaic of wetlands, lakes and woods. Nearly 20 miles of trails wind through the park, which also features a 6-acre beach.

PHOTOGRAPHS: JOHN NOLTNER

Grand Rapids boasts one of the nation's top culinary schools and a local-food scene that rivals any in the region.

Frederik Meijer Gardens' *The American Horse* is based on drawings by Leonardo da Vinci.

# BALINESE DUCK

*Cygnus 27 features a globally inspired menu. One of the tropical specialties is this wonderfully spiced entree that showcases the richness of duck and macadamia nuts, contrasting perfectly with a lively pineapple salsa. Even better, it's as easy to prepare as it is pretty and flavorful.*

Prep: 1 hour  Marinate: 4 hours  Broil: 12 minutes  Stand: 5 minutes

PHOTOGRAPHS: KEVIN J. MIYAZAKI/REDUX

4   6- to 7-ounce fresh or frozen boneless domestic duck breasts
1   cup finely chopped macadamia nuts
1   cup ground palm sugar or packed brown sugar
5   shallots, halved and thinly sliced
3   to 4 fresh red Thai (bird's eye) chile peppers (see Chef Tip, page 148), seeded and finely chopped
¼   cup snipped fresh cilantro
2   tablespoons kosher salt

2   tablespoons ground coriander
2   tablespoons coarse ground black pepper
2   tablespoons grated fresh ginger
5   cloves garlic, minced
1   teaspoon ground turmeric
3   cups hot cooked rice
    Root Vegetable Mash (recipe follows)
    Fruit Salsa (see recipe, page 147)
    Bok choy leaves, steamed (optional)

**1.** Thaw duck, if frozen. Trim and discard fat from duck.

**2.** In a medium bowl, combine macadamia nuts, palm sugar, shallots, chile peppers, cilantro, salt, coriander, black pepper, ginger, garlic and turmeric. Spoon nut mixture on top of duck; press down gently to coat. Place duck in a 12x7x2-inch (2-quart rectangular) baking dish. Cover and marinate in the refrigerator for 4 hours.

**3.** Transfer the duck to the unheated rack of a broiler pan. Broil about 7 inches from the heat for 12 to 15 minutes or until an instant-read thermometer registers 155°. (Or transfer duck to a shallow roasting pan. Roast in a 425° oven about 15 minutes or until an instant-read thermometer registers 155°.) Cover loosely with foil and let stand for 5 minutes before slicing (the temperature of the duck will rise 5° during standing time). Slice duck.

**4.** For each serving, spoon hot cooked rice onto a warm dinner plate. Top with duck slices. Serve with Root Vegetable Mash and Fruit Salsa. If you like, garnish with steamed bok choy leaves. **Makes 4 servings.**

**Root Vegetable Mash:** Peel 8 ounces taro root or parsnips, 8 ounces baking potato and 8 ounces yam. Cut into 2-inch pieces. Peel 12 cloves garlic. Place a steamer basket into a Dutch oven; add water to just below basket. Bring water to boiling. Place the vegetables and garlic in the steamer basket. Cover and steam for 15 to 20 minutes or until vegetables are very tender. Carefully remove steamer basket from Dutch oven.

In a large saucepan, melt 1 teaspoon butter over medium heat. Add 1 cup sliced green onion. Cook and stir about 5 minutes or until tender. Slowly add 1 cup whipping cream to the onion mixture, stirring constantly. Bring just to boiling over medium heat. Boil gently about 10 minutes or until the mixture is reduced by half.

Add the steamed vegetables. Mash with a potato masher. Stir in 3 tablespoons melted butter. Season to taste with kosher salt and freshly ground black pepper. Serve warm. Makes about 3½ cups.

Sea scallops à la plancha is inspired by classic French cuisine. *(Below)* The dining room opens off the opulent lobby of the Amway Grand Plaza.

# SEA SCALLOPS À LA PLANCHA

*"My recipe celebrates Michigan's late-summer bounty of tomatoes and zucchini flavors that always make me think of Provence in the south of France," reflects Amway Grand Plaza chef Christian Madsen. A plancha is a type of griddle used in Spain use a cast-iron skillet.* Prep: 45 minutes  Chill: 8 hours  Cook: 3

8  to 10 fresh or frozen sea scallops (1 pound)
1  tablespoon olive oil
¾  teaspoon sea salt or ¼ teaspoon salt
¼  teaspoon freshly ground black pepper
   Tomato Consommé (recipe follows)
   Provençal Vegetable Ratatouille (see recipe, page 148)
   Fresh herbs, such as watercress, basil, oregano, rosemary
      and/or chives (optional)

**1.** Thaw the scallops, if frozen. Rinse scallops; pat dry with paper towels. Rub all surfaces of scallops with oil; sprinkle with salt and pepper.
**2.** Heat a large cast-iron skillet or heavy skillet over high or medium-high heat until very hot. Carefully add scallops. Cook for 3 to 4 minutes or until the scallops are opaque, turning once halfway through cooking.
**3.** For each serving, spoon some of the warm Tomato Consommé into a warm shallow bowl. Place a spoonful of warm Provençal Vegetable Ratatouille in center. Place a scallop on each side of the ratatouille. If you like, garnish with fresh herbs. Serve immediately.
**Makes 4 or 5 appetizer servings.**

**Tomato Consommé:** In a food processor or blender, combine 10 medium roma tomatoes, halved; ¼ cup firmly packed fresh basil leaves; 1 tablespoon tomato paste; 1 teaspoon kosher salt or ½ teaspoon salt; 1 clove garlic, halved; ½ teaspoon fresh thyme leaves and ¼ teaspoon freshly ground black pepper. Cover and process or blend until almost smooth. Line a colander or sieve with two layers of 100-percent-cotton cheesecloth. Set colander in a large glass bowl (bottom of colander needs to be suspended over bowl by at least 3 inches). Pour tomato mixture into colander. Cover and let drain in the refrigerator for 8 to 24 hours. Before serving, pour tomato juice from bowl into a small saucepan (mixture will be clear); discard tomato mixture in colander. Bring to boiling. Remove from heat; keep warm. Makes about 1¾ cups.

## Grand Rapids' masterpiece

Natural beauty and world-class art combine in elegant harmony within Frederik Meijer Gardens & Sculpture Park, a 132-acre preserve of wetlands, woods, meadows and gardens northeast of Grand Rapids.

Planned as an innovative approach to public gardens and opened in 1995, Meijer gained international fame in 1998 with the unveiling of Nina Akamu's striking 24-foot-tall bronze *American Horse (see page 23)*. In addition to the Leonardo da Vinci-inspired work, the Sculpture Park contains some 150 works of art by more than 30 renowned artists including Alexander Liberman's *Aria (above)*.

Within the preserve, visitors browse Michigan's largest tropical conservatory, one of the nation's largest children's gardens and the Michigan farm garden. Summers, the outdoor amphitheater hosts big-name live-music concerts.

PHOTOGRAPHS: JOHN NOLTNER (OPPOSITE) KEVIN J. MIYAZAKI/REDUX

# CHOCOLATE SOUFFLÉ

*Chocolate gives this Amway Grand Plaza dessert its deep color and flavor. It's made even more irresistible with a glittering orange layer of gelée (juice and gelatin) and crème fraîche. Chef Christian Madsen recommends serving this French-inspired treat with a cup of freshly brewed espresso.*

Prep: 50 minutes  Bake: 30 minutes  Cool: 45 minutes
Freeze: 1 hour plus 8 hours  Stand: 5 minutes

| | |
|---|---|
| 9 | egg yolks |
| 5 | egg whites |
| 1 | cup butter |
| 12 | ounces semisweet chocolate, chopped |
| 3½ | cups sugar |

| | |
|---|---|
| 4 | envelopes unflavored gelatin |
| 6 | cups unsweetened blood orange juice or orange juice with pulp plus 10 drops red food coloring |
| | Crème fraîche or sweetened whipped cream |
| | Blood oranges or oranges, peeled and sectioned |

**1.** Allow egg yolks, egg whites and butter to stand at room temperature for 30 minutes.

**2.** Meanwhile, place chocolate in a large microwave-safe bowl. Microwave, uncovered, on 70 percent power (medium-high) for 1 minute; stir. Microwave on medium-high for 1 to 2 minutes more or until chocolate is melted and smooth, stirring every 15 seconds. Let stand to cool slightly. Line a 13x9x2-inch baking pan with foil, extending the foil over edges of the baking pan. Set aside.

**3.** For soufflé: In a medium bowl, beat egg yolks and ¼ cup of the sugar with an electric mixer on medium to medium-high speed about 10 minutes or until thick and lemon colored; set aside. In a very large bowl, beat butter on medium speed about 2 minutes or until light and fluffy. Add slightly warm chocolate; beat until combined. Fold the egg yolk mixture into the chocolate mixture.

**4.** Thoroughly wash and dry beaters. In a large bowl, beat egg whites on medium speed about 1 minute or until soft peaks form (tips curl). Gradually add ¼ cup of the sugar, 1 tablespoon at a time, beating on high speed about 4 minutes more or until mixture forms stiff, glossy peaks (tips stand straight) and sugar dissolves (rub a small amount between two fingers; it should feel completely smooth).

**5.** Gently fold half of the stiffly beaten egg whites into chocolate mixture. Gently fold remaining egg whites into chocolate-egg white mixture. Transfer to the prepared pan.

**6.** Bake in a 325° oven for 30 to 35 minutes or until a knife inserted off-center comes out clean (soufflé will fall slightly as it cools). Remove from oven; cool in pan on a wire rack for 45 minutes. Cover; freeze for 1 hour.

**7.** Meanwhile, in a large saucepan, stir together the remaining 3 cups sugar and the gelatin; stir in 3 cups of the blood orange juice. Heat and stir until gelatin dissolves. Remove from heat. Stir in the remaining 3 cups blood orange juice. Pour orange juice mixture over frozen soufflé. Cover and freeze for 8 to 24 hours.

**8.** To serve, using the edges of the foil, lift chocolate soufflé out of pan. Let stand for 5 minutes. Trim edges; cut lengthwise into three rows. Cut crosswise in four even rows. Cut each piece in half to form two triangles.

**9.** For each serving, place a chocolate soufflé triangle in the center of a chilled dessert plate. Top with crème fraîche. Garnish with orange sections. **Makes 24 servings.**

PHOTOGRAPHS: KEVIN J. MIYAZAKI/REDUX

# Creative Tastes
# in Traverse City

IT'S SURPRISING REALLY that Traverse City hasn't tried to copyright the phrase "creative dining." After all, this vacation hub on the shore of Grand Traverse Bay seems to claim as many innovative chefs and dining options as classic vacation experiences and eateries. These leading-edge chefs draw on one of the richest local food and wine scenes anywhere (see "Pure Inspiration" beginning on page 50).

"What makes this a unique area is that it's a destination resort spot with a great deal of agricultural diversity," explains Fred Laughlin director of Traverse City's Great Lakes Culinary Institute. Which is the academic way of saying that chefs love fresh ingredients, and they're not immune to the allure of sugar-sand beaches.

The region's bounty is legendary: Lake Michigan produces boatloads of whitefish, lake trout and chubs. The lakeshore climate ensures hundreds of thousands of cherry trees flourish on hillsides. Lettuces, asparagus and other vegetables grow with organic care on dozens of small farm plots. Prized mushrooms hide in shady forests. Rich pastures support dairy

Once a commercial fishing village, Leland's historic Fishtown boasts a wide array of shops, galleries and restaurants. (*Left*) Fresh-from-the-orchard cherries.

FOUR FABULOUS PLATES

### Lake@The Cooks' House
The second-oldest building in Traverse City houses this local favorite where regional fish stars. What could be better than walleye accented with slow-cooked fennel and caramelized onions?

### Land@ Trattoria Stella
Extensive but constantly changing, the spring menu always includes tender local-grown asparagus flavorfully char-grilled and served with a poached egg, crostini and hollandaise.

### Fusion@Hanna Bistro
The blueberry-feta salad comes dressed with Blueberry Balsamic Vinaigrette from Fustini's in Petoskey; the crumb tart features local fruit and a scoop of bourbon-vanilla ice cream.

cows that provide milk for cheeses and ice cream. More than two dozen vineyards produce world-class wines. Matched with those ingredients are a host of culinary entrepreneurs who have created a cornucopia of unforgettable foods in and near the community. Among them are Trattoria Stella and The Cooks' House in Traverse City, where the menus change daily depending on what's fresh locally (chalkboards at both list several dozen area growers and producers they rely on).

"Traverse City is on the food map now," says Stella chef Myles Anton. Myles, recently honored as a 2010 James Beard best chef semifinalist for the Great Lakes region, adds, "The farm-to-table movement is huge here."

## TASTES GUIDE

A popular vacation destination, Traverse City has been attracting visitors for more than 100 years. Motels with private beaches line the shore while inventive restaurants lead the way with authentic food. Recreation abounds with area wineries, golf courses and shopping. For more ideas, information and links, visit michigan.org.

**AERIE** A luxury spa, 54 holes of championship golf and a shopping gallery are among the attractions at

### Les Oeufs@Chez Peres
Daily brunch at this French-style bistro stars eggs served truffled with Gruyère, as an omelet of Leelanau cheese and herbs, with gravlax and hollandaise and, of course, as eggs Benedict.

PHOTOGRAPHS: KEVIN J. MIYAZAKI/REDUX. (OPPOSITE, FROM LEFT) KEVIN J. MIYAZAKI/REDUX, BOB STEFKO

In the heart of downtown Suttons Bay, Gusto! Ristorante serves up classic Italian with creative twists, as well as American fare, in a casual, family-friendly setting.

Grand Traverse Resort & Spa with a distinctive glass tower overlooking Grand Traverse Bay northeast of Traverse City in Acme. On the tower's 16th floor, lovely Aerie Restaurant features a menu centered on local ingredients and serves Michigan wines.

**CHEZ PERES** In downtown Traverse City and until recently called Patisserie Amie, this bistro's French fare includes brunch items such as truffled eggs and salmon crepes. Breads and pastries crowd the bakery case.

**CRAFT BREWS** Traverse City-crafted brews range from porters and stouts at North Peak Brewing Company and Kilkenny's Irish Public House to pale ales at Right Brain Brewery and Belgian-style wheat ale at Mackinaw Brewing Company.

**FUSTINI'S OILS & VINEGARS** Sold in Ann Arbor, Traverse City, Petoskey and Holland, Fustini's olive oil is infused with real ingredients like herbs, citrus and mushrooms. In the tasting room, create your own

Built in 1870, Old Mission Point Lighthouse caps the tip of Old Mission Peninsula. (*Right*) Grocer's Daughter's indulgent dark chocolate bars topped with nuts and cranberries.

PHOTOGRAPHS: (FROM LEFT) ROB STEFKO, KEVIN J. MIYAZAKI/REDUX

combination and take home a bottle.

**GUSTO! RISTORANTE** In Suttons Bay, chef-prepared Italian dishes range from pan-seared calamari to old-school spaghetti and meatballs. Try the pizza baked in a stone oven or salad with from-scratch dressing.

**LOBDELL'S RESTAURANT** Students at the Great Lakes Culinary Institute prepare and serve mushroom prosciutto crepes, pumpkin-walnut crusted walleye and other savory creations at this teaching restaurant along West Grand Traverse Bay.

**MARTHA'S LEELANAU TABLE** Everything is made from scratch at this breakfast and lunch spot in Suttons Bay.

**MOOMERS** This Traverse City spot has taken the vacation area's love affair with ice cream to new levels. Flavors such as Sticky Bun, White Chocolate Oreo and Pumpkin Roll are among the revolving menu of more than 100.

**RED GINGER** Thai curry, lobster tempura, sushi and extend-your-pinky elegant martinis star.

**SLABTOWN BURGERS** Handmade burgers and hand-cut fries come in a brown paper bag; located downtown.

**SOUL HOLE** New and becoming a Traverse City locals' favorite, this is the place for po'boys, shrimp and grits, and bourbon pecan pie.

**THE VILLAGE AT GRAND TRAVERSE COMMONS** One mile west of downtown in several restored 1880s buildings, the commons is home to Trattoria Stella, the Pleasanton Brick Oven Bakery, Left Foot Charley winery, Cuppa Joe, the Underground Cheesecake Company, plus other food shops, galleries and boutiques.

**ZAKEY RESTAURANT** Downtown Traverse City has experienced many firsts in the past decade. Now, comes Middle Eastern cuisine. In this intimate restaurant (the name means "delicious"), patrons can watch owner Nabiel Musleh grill kabobs in the open kitchen while a belly dancer gyrates to traditional Middle Eastern music on Saturday nights.

## BETWEEN MEALS

**BEACHES** Stake claim to some sand at public beaches along Grand Traverse Bay, including those at Bryant and Clinch parks and the West End Beach with plenty of parking.

**BEACH RESORTS** From Bayshore Resort to Tamarack Lodge, choose among dozens of waterside properties in and near Traverse City, most with their own beach.

**SHANTY CREEK RESORTS** A $10 million renovation has transformed the Lakeview Hotel & Conference Center, the heart of this 4,500-acre golf-ski complex near tiny Bellaire (25 miles northeast of Traverse City).

Some lushly appointed rooms look out on Lake Bellaire. Framed by a two-story wall of windows, the Lakeview Restaurant has the same view. Time your reservation for sunset, and indulge in a signature steak or specialty such as osso bucco. Sports fans head to Ivan's Mountain Side Grill for pizza and a pint.

## GROCER'S DAUGHTER CHOCOLATE

Mimi Wheeler is living her culinary dream as a second career. The transplanted Denmark native and retired Michigan social worker now spends her days in the small lime-green Grocer's Daughter shop in tiny Empire (20 miles west of Traverse City) creating widely celebrated bon bons, truffles and caramels.

"I grew up in a culture that reveres chocolate," she says, adding, "I like to experiment."

Among the chocolates on Mimi's brimming candy counter are many accented with familiar flavors such as cherry, almond and espresso. Others offer decidedly untraditional tastes including basil, rosemary and cardamom. Mimi incorporates her homegrown herbs fresh from the garden.

"Northern Michigan in the summer is the most amazing place. From the blue skies to the sandy beaches to lush forest trails, you are surrounded with nature at its best."

— JIMMY SCHMIDT, RATTLESNAKE CLUB

Windsurfing on Lake Michigan, Sleeping Bear Dunes National Lakeshore.

# WHITEFISH CAKES WITH PARSNIP FRITES

*What gives Hanna Bistro's chef Carrie Trogan's dish its extraordinary taste? Fresh corn and portobellos grilled over an outdoor fire. The smoked flavor adds depth. The parsnip frites add a touch of sweetness and crunch.* Prep: 1½ hours  Bake: 6 minutes plus 10 minutes  Grill: 15 minutes  Chill: 1 hour  Cook: 5 minutes per batch

---

3¼ to 3½ pounds fresh or frozen skinless lake whitefish, lake perch, haddock or flounder fillets
1 tablespoon Old Bay seasoning
2 fresh portobello mushrooms
2 cups fresh or frozen whole kernel corn
1 egg, lightly beaten
1¼ cups fine dry bread crumbs
¾ cup finely chopped red sweet pepper
½ cup finely chopped celery
½ cup finely chopped green onion
⅓ cup mayonnaise
⅓ cup coarse ground mustard
3 tablespoons snipped fresh parsley

2 teaspoons finely shredded lemon peel
2 tablespoons lemon juice
1½ teaspoons snipped fresh rosemary
1½ teaspoons snipped fresh thyme
1 teaspoon freshly ground black pepper
½ teaspoon kosher salt or ¼ teaspoon salt
¼ teaspoon bottled hot pepper sauce
¼ cup vegetable oil
1 7-ounce jar roasted red sweet peppers, drained
4 cups hot cooked brown rice
Parsnip Frites (see recipe, page 141)
Small fresh basil leaves
Fresh parsley sprigs

---

**1.** Thaw fish, if frozen. Rinse fish; pat dry with paper towels. Sprinkle with Old Bay seasoning. Cut fish crosswise into ¾-inch slices. Place fish in a single layer in a greased shallow baking pan. Bake in a 450° oven for 6 to 10 minutes or until fish begins to flake when tested with a fork. Remove from oven. Set aside.
**2.** Cut off mushroom stems even with caps; discard stems. If you like, remove gills. Lightly rinse mushroom caps. Gently pat dry with paper towels; finely chop mushrooms.
**3.** To create a perforated pan: Use the tip of a small sharp knife to punch

several holes in the bottom of a 13x9x3-inch (3-quart rectangular) disposable foil pan. Add mushrooms and corn.
**4.** For a charcoal grill: Place foil pan on the rack of an uncovered grill directly over low coals. Grill for 15 to 20 minutes or until corn is tender, stirring once halfway through grilling. (For a gas grill: Preheat grill. Reduce heat to low. Place foil pan on grill rack over heat. Cover and grill as directed.) Set aside.
**5.** For fish cakes: In a large bowl, combine the egg, bread crumbs, sweet pepper, celery, green onion,

mayonnaise, mustard, the 3 tablespoons parsley, lemon peel, lemon juice, rosemary, thyme, black pepper, salt and hot pepper sauce. Stir in corn mixture. Flake fish; stir into corn mixture until well mixed.
**6.** For each fish cake, use a 3x2½-inch ring mold or a 3x2-inch round cookie or biscuit cutter and pack ¾ cup of the fish mixture firmly and evenly into the mold. Unmold fish cake onto a baking sheet lined with waxed paper. Cover and chill for at least 1 hour or up to 8 hours.
*Continued on page 140*

PHOTOGRAPHS: KEVIN J. MIYAZAKI/REDUX

# GRILLED ASPARAGUS WITH POACHED EGG

*Looking for another way to serve tender spring asparagus? Try this luxurious recipe from Trattoria Stella where diners love the fresh-tasting dishes. What's the secret? It's simple. Owner Amanda Danielson confesses, "We make nearly everything in-house and use local produce."* Prep: 1 hour  Grill: 4 minutes  Cook: 3 minutes

24  fresh asparagus spears (about 1 pound)
2  tablespoons olive oil
4  cups water
2  tablespoons vinegar
4  eggs
4  1-inch slices sourdough French or Italian bread, toasted, or 4 English muffins, split and toasted
    Lemon Zabaglione Hollandaise Sauce (see recipe, page 148)
    Snipped fresh Italian (flat-leaf) parsley

**1.** For asparagus: Snap off and discard fibrous stem ends of asparagus; rinse and drain well. If desired, scrape off scales. Lightly coat asparagus with oil. For a charcoal grill: Place asparagus crosswise on the rack of an uncovered grill directly over medium coals. Grill for 4 to 6 minutes or until crisp-tender, turning spears occasionally. (For a gas grill: Preheat grill. Reduce heat to medium. Place asparagus crosswise on grill rack over heat. Cover and grill as above.) Remove from grill; cover with foil to keep warm.
**2.** For poached eggs: Lightly grease a large skillet. Add the water and vinegar. Bring to boiling; reduce heat to simmering (bubbles should begin to break the surface). Break one of the eggs into a 1-cup measuring cup with

a handle. Holding lip of cup as close to the water as possible, gently slide egg into simmering water, being careful not to break the yolk. Repeat with the remaining eggs, allowing each egg an equal amount of space. Simmer eggs, uncovered, for 3 to 5 minutes or until whites are completely set and yolks begin to thicken but are still soft. Remove eggs with a slotted spoon and place them in a large pan of warm water to keep warm. Just before serving, remove eggs with a slotted spoon and place them on paper towels to drain.
**3.** For each serving, place one slice bread in center of a warm plate. Top with six asparagus spears and a drained poached egg. Spoon Lemon Zabaglione Hollandaise Sauce over egg. Sprinkle with parsley. **Makes 4 servings.**

## Carlson's of Fishtown

Smells of maple smoke and fish mingle in a blue haze rising from Fishtown's weathered buildings along Lake Michigan in Leland (about 30 miles northwest of Traverse City). The scents waft from Carlson's Fisheries, where chubs and whitefish are delicately smoked before going on display in a glass case with other freshly caught fish.

The Carlson family has been fishing the waters off Leland since the 1860s.

"I'm generation four," explains Bill Carlson, the tall, white-whiskered family patriarch. "Generations five and six are in the shop."

Chances are good that if you eat a whitefish supper in the Traverse City area, it's a Carlson-caught fish. Carlson's smoked chubs even show up as organic swizzle sticks in the Chubby Mary's served in the bar at Leland's Rick's Cafe.

PHOTOGRAPHS: BOB STEFKO. (OPPOSITE) KEVIN J. MIYAZAKI/REDUX

Since 1872, the South Manitou Island Light has warned of the treacherous waters off the island that's now part of Sleeping Bear Dunes National Lakeshore. *(Above)* Walleye with slow-cooked fennel.

# WALLEYE WITH SLOW-COOKED FENNEL

*Chef Eric Patterson showcases walleye drawn from nearby waters on his Cooks' House menu. Locally grown onion and fennel mellow with slow cooking and accent the slightly sweet flavor of the fish. Serve it with crisp salad greens.*

Prep: 40 minutes  Roast: 45 minutes  Cook: 20 minutes

4   6- to 8-ounce fresh or frozen boneless walleye pike fillets with skin, catfish fillets or other fish fillets ($\frac{1}{2}$ to $\frac{3}{4}$ inch thick)
1   large fennel bulb
1   tablespoon olive oil
$\frac{1}{4}$   teaspoon kosher salt or salt
$\frac{1}{8}$   teaspoon freshly ground black pepper
3   cloves garlic, coarsely chopped
2   fresh thyme sprigs
$\frac{1}{4}$   cup butter

2   large yellow onions, halved lengthwise and thinly sliced
    Kosher salt or salt
    Freshly ground black pepper
$\frac{1}{4}$   cup olive oil
1   shallot, minced
2   tablespoons rice vinegar
1   tablespoon spicy brown mustard
$\frac{1}{4}$   teaspoon kosher salt or salt
1   tablespoon olive oil

**1.** Thaw fish, if frozen. Rinse fish and pat dry with paper towels. Cover and chill until ready to fry.

**2.** For fennel: Cut off and discard fennel stalks. Remove any wilted outer layers and cut a thin slice from the base of the bulb. Wash fennel; cut lengthwise into quarters. Fold a 36x18-inch piece of heavy foil in half to make an 18-inch square. Place fennel in center of foil. Drizzle fennel with the 1 tablespoon olive oil. Sprinkle with $\frac{1}{4}$ teaspoon salt and the $\frac{1}{8}$ teaspoon pepper. Top with garlic and thyme. Bring up two opposite edges of foil; seal with a double fold. Fold remaining ends to completely enclose fennel, leaving space for steam to build. Place in a shallow roasting pan.

Roast in a 350° oven about 45 minutes or until fennel is tender. Remove from oven; uncover and let cool.

**3.** For onions: In a large skillet, melt butter over medium-low heat. Add onions. Sprinkle with additional salt and pepper. Cook, uncovered, for 20 to 30 minutes or until onions are tender, stirring frequently. Remove from heat; cover with foil to keep warm.

**4.** For vinaigrette: In a bowl, whisk together the $\frac{1}{4}$ cup olive oil, the shallot, rice vinegar, mustard and $\frac{1}{4}$ teaspoon salt until combined. Set aside.

**5.** For fish: Score the fish skin by cutting narrow slits at $\frac{1}{4}$-inch intervals on top of the fish, cutting through skin and just into the flesh (scoring helps make the fish crispy). In a very large

nonstick skillet, heat the 1 tablespoon olive oil over medium-high heat. When a drop of water sizzles in skillet, add two of the fish fillets, skin sides down. Fry about 4 minutes or until golden brown and fish is three-quarters cooked (fish will be white three-quarters of the way up the side). Using a wide spatula, carefully turn fish; fry about 1 minute more or until fish begins to flake when tested with a fork. Remove from skillet and drain on paper towels. Keep warm in a 300° oven while frying remaining fish, adding additional oil, if necessary.

**6.** For each serving, place onions in the center of a plate. Top with fish and fennel. Whisk vinaigrette; drizzle over fish and fennel. **Makes 4 servings.**

PHOTOGRAPHS: KEVIN J. MIYAZAKI/REDUX; (OPPOSITE, FROM TOP) KEVIN J. MIYAZAKI/REDUX, JASON LINDSEY

*(From left)* Evans Street Station brings diners near and far to tiny Tecumseh. Seafood risotto at The Common Grill in Chelsea.

## Smaller-Town Food and Travel Surprises

INNOVATIVE CHEFS and local cuisine aren't unique to Michigan cities. Some of the state's best food is found in small towns.

For delicious proof, spread your napkin at Evans Street Station in Tecumseh (population: 8,700; 30 miles southwest of Ann Arbor) and The Common Grill in Chelsea (pop: 4,400; 18 miles northwest of Ann Arbor). Up North, Hermann's boasts fine dining in Cadillac (pop: 10,200; 200 miles north of Ann Arbor).

In Tecumseh, celebrated chef Alan Merhar's exhibition-style kitchen opens onto a comfortably elegant dining room within the former Evans Street fire station.

From roasted duck breast to the haricots verts, the sophisticated menu at this 10-year-old restaurant relies mostly on local ingredients. And just about everything is made in-house from scratch, including breads, soup stocks, sauces and desserts.

"We are proud to be leaders in Michigan's local-food movement," says Beth Kennedy, who shares Evans Street ownership with her parents and the Michigan-born chef.

Another Michigan native, chef Craig Common, plied his talents across the nation before returning at the behest of the father of actor Jeff Daniels, who had opened The Purple Rose Theatre in his hometown of Chelsea.

"The idea was simply to have a place for people to have a great meal before or after the play," Craig recalls.

The duo re-created a Chelsea department store building as a bright, contemporary bistro. In his kitchen, Craig pays homage to Michigan with a palette of local ingredients and with dishes such as pan-fried walleye in a black walnut crust and the warm Michigan peach upside-down cake.

Austrian-born chef Hermann Suhs, who has cooked around the globe, settled in his wife's hometown of Cadillac a little more than two decades ago. Hermann's casually elegant restaurant has become an institution known for unfailing hospitality and from-scratch sauces and dressings.

### TASTES GUIDE

Top chefs and their restaurants await in smaller towns with charming business districts (Tecumseh), mini versions of hip college towns (Chelsea) and an abundance of wildlife and national forests (Cadillac).

PHOTOGRAPHS: KEVIN J. MIYAZAKI/REDUX

*(From left)* Lakes dot 11,000-acre Pinckney State Recreation Area near Chelsea. Cheers! at Evans Street Station in Tecumseh.

**BOULEVARD MARKET** The downtown Tecumseh market is noted for its extensive selection of wine, beer and gourmet goodies, as well as fresh breads and artisanal cheeses, made on-site at Four Corners Creamery.

**CHELSEA FARMERS MARKET** Held downtown on Saturdays May through October, the market showcases Michigan produce, eggs, honey, meat and poultry plus flowers and crafts.

**CHELSEA HOUSE VICTORIAN INN** Behind Chelsea's Purple Rose Theatre, the lovingly restored 1881 Queen Anne house features four guest rooms and the Carriage House suite.

**CHELSEA MILLING COMPANY** Purveyor of "Jiffy" Mix, the mill has been grinding flour for more than 120 years.

**PENTAMERE WINERY** Regional character is the hallmark of the reds and whites crafted at this Tecumseh winery and tasting room.

**THE SWEET SHOP** Homemade chocolates and fudge, made the old-fashioned way, have been the foundation of this downtown Cadillac shop for more than 50 years. You can also buy Michigan maple syrup.

**TECUMSEH FARMERS MARKET** Saturdays May through October, soaps, pottery and homemade pies complement the booths of vegetables, herbs, flowers, eggs and honey.

**ZOU ZOU'S CAFE** Born in France, owner Marie-Ann Fody brings international flair to this downtown Chelsea cafe serving buttery brioche and fluffy quiches under a pressed-tin ceiling.

## BETWEEN MEALS

**PURPLE ROSE THEATRE** Intimate seating, reasonably priced tickets and plays highlighting its middle-American roots make this nonprofit Chelsea theater a popular destination.

**THREE FABULOUS PLATES**

### Surf@Common Grill
Walleye, lake perch and whitefish achieve the same elegance at this Chelsea spot as the sea bass and halibut.

### Turf@Evans Street
Roasted duck breast arrives with peas, applewood-smoked bacon and braised fingerling potatoes at this former fire station in downtown Tecumseh.

### Old World Flair@ Hermann's
Choose from rack of lamb à la Provençale, chicken breast piccata and crisp fried German potato pancakes in one of Cadillac's fine-dining restaurants.

# BANANA CREAM CHOCOLATE TART

*Under a cloud of vanilla whipped cream, slices of banana nestle in filling infused with white chocolate, and a buttery shell rests in a puddle of bittersweet chocolate. "My daughter loves this dessert," says chef Craig Common, owner of The Common Grill in Chelsea.*

Prep: 1 hour  Chill: 1 hour  Bake: 20 minutes

1 cup sugar
⅓ cup cornstarch
3 cups milk
1 4- to 5-inch vanilla bean
8 egg yolks, lightly beaten
1 cup white baking pieces
2 tablespoons butter

½ cup semisweet chocolate pieces, melted
 Chocolate Pastry Tart Shells (recipe follows)
2 medium bananas, sliced or chopped
 Vanilla Bean Whipped Cream (see recipe, page 150)
 Hot Fudge Sauce (see recipe, page 150)
 Powdered sugar

**1.** For pastry cream: In a heavy medium saucepan, combine sugar and cornstarch. Stir in milk. Using a knife, slit vanilla bean lengthwise. Using knife tip, scrape out seeds; reserve about one-fourth of the seeds for Vanilla Bean Whipped Cream. Add remaining seeds to milk mixture. Cook and stir over medium heat until thickened and bubbly. Cook and stir for 2 minutes more. Remove pan from heat.
**2.** Gradually stir 1 cup of the milk mixture into egg yolks. Return egg mixture to milk mixture in saucepan. Bring just to boiling; reduce heat. Cook and stir for 2 minutes more. Remove pan from heat. Strain mixture through a wire mesh sieve. Stir white baking pieces and butter into strained mixture; continue stirring until baking pieces melt and mixture is smooth.

Spoon pastry cream into a bowl. Cover surface with plastic wrap; chill for at least 1 hour or up to 8 hours (do not stir).
**3.** For chocolate shards: Line a 15x10x1-inch baking pan with parchment paper. Pour melted semisweet chocolate into prepared baking pan, spreading evenly. Let stand at room temperature or chill in the refrigerator until set. Break into large pieces.
**4.** Spoon one-fourth of pastry cream into each Chocolate Pastry Tart Shell. Divide bananas and Vanilla Bean Whipped Cream among tart shells.
**5.** For each serving, spoon some of the Hot Fudge Sauce on a dessert plate. Top with a filled tart shell. Garnish with chocolate shards and dust with powdered sugar.
**Makes 4 tarts (8 servings).**

**Chocolate Pastry Tart Shells:** Cut 2 tablespoons cold unsalted butter into ¼-inch cubes; freeze for 10 minutes. In a medium bowl, stir together ¾ cup all-purpose flour and ½ teaspoon sugar. Using a pastry blender, cut in butter cubes until pieces are pea size. Sprinkle 1 tablespoon cold whipping cream over part of the flour mixture; gently toss with a fork. Push moistened pastry to side of bowl. Repeat moistening flour mixture, using 1 tablespoon more cold whipping cream. Remove dough from bowl; shape into a ball by gently pushing down with the heel of your hand so the mixture comes together. Flatten into a disk. Cover dough disk with plastic wrap or place in a plastic bag and seal; chill for 20 to 30 minutes or until dough is easy to handle.
*Continued on page 150*

# GRILLED LAMB CHOPS

*Chef Alan Merhar tempts diners nightly with his contemporary cuisine at Evans Street Station in Tecumseh. This lamb entree with Middle Eastern fattoush and garlicky hummus is one example. When Alan prepares the recipe, he prefers to cut his own chops from a rack of lamb. You'll find buying the rib chops precut easier.*

Prep: 45 minutes  Chill: 1 hour  Grill: 12 minutes  Stand: 5 minutes

12  2- to 3-ounce lamb rib chops, cut 1 inch thick
    Sea salt or salt
    Cracked black pepper
 2  lemons, halved and seeded
 2  large pita bread rounds
    Fattoush (recipe follows)
    Hummus (recipe follows)

**1.** Trim fat from chops. Sprinkle both sides of chops with salt and pepper.
**2.** For a charcoal grill: Place chops on the greased rack of an uncovered grill directly over medium coals. Grill to desired doneness, turning once halfway through grilling. (Allow 12 to 14 minutes for medium-rare doneness [145°] or 15 to 17 minutes for medium doneness [160°].) Place lemon halves, cut sides down, on grill rack next to chops during the last 5 minutes of grilling or just until charred. Grill pita bread for 2 to 4 minutes or until lightly toasted, turning once halfway through grilling. (For a gas grill: Preheat grill. Reduce heat to medium. Place chops, then lemon and pita bread on greased grill rack over heat. Cover and grill as above.)
**3.** Remove the chops, lemon and pita bread from grill. Let chops stand for

5 minutes before serving.
**4.** Cut the pita bread into triangles.
**5.** For each serving, mound some of the Fattoush in the center of a warm dinner plate. Arrange three of the chops and pita triangles on top of Fattoush. Serve with Hummus and lemon halves. **Makes 4 servings.**

**Fattoush:** In a large bowl, combine 1 medium English cucumber, seeded and finely chopped (2 cups); 2 medium tomatoes, seeded and finely chopped (1 cup); 1 medium red sweet pepper, finely chopped (1 cup); 1 medium yellow sweet pepper, finely chopped (1 cup) and 1 small red onion, finely chopped (⅓ cup). Toss gently to combine.
   For dressing: In a screw-top jar, combine ⅓ cup olive oil; ¼ cup lemon juice; 3 tablespoons snipped fresh

Italian (flat-leaf) parsley; 2 tablespoons snipped fresh mint; 3 cloves garlic, minced; 1 teaspoon sea salt or ½ teaspoon salt and ¼ teaspoon freshly ground black pepper. Cover and shake well. Pour dressing over vegetable mixture, tossing to mix. Cover and chill for at least 1 hour or up to 4 hours. Makes about 4 cups.

**Hummus:** Drain one 15-ounce can garbanzo beans (chickpeas), reserving liquid. Rinse beans in a colander; drain well. In a food processor or blender, combine garbanzo beans, 2 tablespoons of the reserved bean liquid, ½ cup tahini (sesame seed paste), ⅓ cup lemon juice and 4 cloves garlic, minced. Cover and process or blend until almost smooth. If mixture is too thick, add a little more reserved bean liquid. Makes 1¾ cups.

PHOTOGRAPHS: KEVIN J. MIYAZAKI/REDUX

# ESTERHÁZY SCHNITTEN

*Chef Hermann Suhs from Hermann's in Cadillac was born and raised near Vienna where he learned to create pastries. A classic Austrian dessert, Esterházy Schnitten sports a herringbone pattern (chevron) design on top. A rich vanilla filling and apricot preserves alternate with layers of fondant icing and chocolate.* Prep: 45 minutes  Bake: 12 minutes  Cool: 10 minutes
Stand: 15 minutes plus 15 minutes Chill: 2 hours

 5  egg whites
1½  cups whole almonds
 ½  cup fine dry bread crumbs
 ⅓  cup all-purpose flour
 ⅛  teaspoon ground cinnamon
 ½  teaspoon vanilla
 ¾  cup sugar
 1  tablespoon butter, melted and cooled
 1  cup apricot preserves
    Vanilla Mousse (see recipe, page 151)
 1  tablespoon water
 1  ounce semisweet chocolate, chopped
 ¼  teaspoon shortening
    Fondant Icing (see recipe, page 151)
    Whipped cream (optional)

**1.** In a large bowl, allow egg whites to stand at room temperature for 30 minutes. Meanwhile, grease the bottom of a 15x10x1-inch baking pan. Line pan with waxed paper; grease and lightly flour pan. Set pan aside.
**2.** In a food processor, place half of the almonds. Cover and process until almonds are very finely ground but still dry (not oily). Transfer the ground nuts to a medium bowl. Repeat with remaining almonds. Stir bread crumbs, flour and cinnamon into ground nuts; mix well. Set aside.

**3.** Add vanilla to egg whites. Beat with an electric mixer on medium speed until soft peaks form (tips curl). Gradually add sugar, about 2 tablespoons at a time, beating until stiff peaks form (tips stand straight).
**4.** Gently fold the nut mixture into egg white mixture. Gradually pour butter in a thin stream over the egg white mixture, folding in gently. Spread the batter evenly in the prepared pan.
*Continued on page 151*

*Continued on page 151*

## International flair

Chef Hermann Suhs was classically trained in Vienna before embarking on a global career that included serving as executive chef at Michigan's Grand Traverse Resort.

In 1985, the chef opened Hermann's European Cafe in his wife's hometown. Suddenly, a lot of motorists on busy US-131 decided to make detours into Cadillac.

Why? The rich, creamy morel soup is reason enough. But Hermann's European Cafe also tempts with a mix of European stalwarts such as Wiener schnitzel, sauerbraten and apple strudel.

Chef looks the part with his white hair, knotted neck kerchief and kitchen tunic. He prowls the dining rooms, stopping at tables to chat and check. "Good?" he queries. Always.

The feast of flavors continues at the neighboring Chef's Deli and Opa's butcher shop and wine store.

PHOTOGRAPHS: KEVIN J. MIYAZAKI/REDUX

Just-picked cherries and blueberries tempt at Fulton Street Farmers Market in Grand Rapids. *(Opposite)* Bob Sutherland samples the wares at Cherry Republic in Glen Arbor.

PHOTOGRAPHS: KEVIN J. MIYAZAKI/REDUX. (OPPOSITE) BOB STEFKO

# {PURE}
# Inspiration

Cherries, blueberries, grapes, asparagus and other homegrown favorites inspire fresh, unique cuisine and wines that are making the culinary world take notice. Come along to farmers markets, you-pick farms, restaurants that rely on the best of this bounty and wineries across the Great Lakes State. Our recipes from these bastions of fresh bring these exceptional flavors home.

*(From left)* Grapes ripen on the vine. Walter and Eileen Brys at Brys Estate Vineyard & Winery on Old Mission Peninsula.

# Vineyards, orchards and more

YOU WON'T FIND a nicer place to eat than the lands along the northwestern Lower Peninsula's Grand and Little Traverse bays. Between meals, there's the lure of sugar-sand beaches that frame Lake Michigan inlets and the trails, beaches and islands of Sleeping Bear Dunes National Lakeshore. Plus, you'll find mile after mile of backroads to explore amid the vineyards and orchards of the Leelanau and Old Mission peninsulas north of Traverse City. Besides concerts, art, festivals and abundant shopping, you're never far from the next quart of cherries at one of the many orchard stands.

The heart of this foodie paradise extends from Traverse City and its peninsulas north 60 miles along the shores of Grand and Little Traverse bays through Charlevoix and Petoskey, a delightfully dense concentration of restaurants fed on the work of a skilled horde of cheese makers, bakers, chocolatiers, wine makers and brewers, vegetable and fruit growers and, of course, a small fleet of commercial Great Lakes anglers. Many of the artisans open their shops and kitchens to visitors.

## TASTES GUIDE

The National Cherry Festival in July draws crowds. Fall foliage brings droves of leaf peepers. Late spring and early summer are pleasant, often overlooked, times to experience this area. For more information, visit michigan.org.

**CHANDLER'S** Tucked behind its venerable parent, Symons General Store, a fixture for more than 100 years now focusing on selling wines, artisan cheese and all manner of bounty from area producers, this hideaway crafts the best and freshest into creative specialties. Guests can dine in the wine cellar.

**CHERRY ORCHARDS** You're never far from one, and in July, the fruit is juicy ripe. Most feature stores. Pick your own at several, including Farmer White's, Gallagher's Farm Market, King Orchards and Rennie Orchards.

**CROOKED TREE BREADWORKS** You can take out granola and scones, but the breads are the stars and pepper Parmesan is the best seller.

**FARMERS MARKETS** The Sara Hardy Downtown Farmers Market convenes Wednesdays and Saturdays throughout the growing season across from Clinch Park, perched high on a hill overlooking vineyards that roll down to the bay.

PHOTOGRAPHS: KEVIN J. MIYAZAKI/REDUX

*(From left)* Freshly picked sweet cherries. Sample more than 100 gourmet cherry products at Cherry Republic in Glen Arbor.

Fresh and local are second nature in the lands along Grand and Little Traverse bays. From cherry stands and chocolate shops to wineries, unique venues seem to pop up around every bend.

**GRAND TRAVERSE PIE COMPANY** The cherry pie is a house favorite, but it's just one of more than three dozen flavors baked at this small Traverse City-based chain. You can also dine in or take out soups, sandwiches and flaky-crust potpies.

**LEELANAU PENINSULA** North of Traverse City, vineyards stripe the hills of the Leelanau and Old Mission peninsulas, basking in the lake-effect climate. The larger and busier of the two peninsulas crooks between Lake Michigan and Grand Traverse Bay and claims more than a dozen wineries

and a scattering of pretty towns that cater to visitors. Black Star Farms, with a tasting room serving award-winning vintages, also has a posh B&B. We loved the Pinot Gris and the fruit dessert wines.

**OLD MISSION PENINSULA** Nearly 20 vineyards nestle among cherry orchards on this smaller strip of land dividing Grand Traverse Bay. Most offer grand water views. Charming Chateau Grand Traverse Inn stands next to its namesake winery and vineyard, northern Michigan's oldest. European-looking Chateau Chantal

Winery and B&B rests on 65 acres near the tip of the peninsula and overlooks both the East and West Grand Traverse bays.

**TERRY'S** Tucked into a Charlevoix side street, this cafe enjoys a loyal local following. It's easy to see why. The menu features classics including rack of lamb and duck, plus an impressive array of local fish.

## BETWEEN MEALS

**CHARLEVOIX** This pretty harbor town, with its bevy of shops, restaurants and lodgings, squeezes nicely between Little Traverse Bay and Lake Charlevoix. Traffic stops obligingly when the bright-blue drawbridge across the Pine River rises on the half hour for ferries to Beaver Island and other vessels parading to Lake Michigan. A paved walkway follows both sides of the channel. The south

PHOTOGRAPHS: (FROM LEFT) KEVIN J. MIYAZAKI/REDUX, BOB STEFKO

path leads to a jaunty red lighthouse at the channel mouth and a neighboring town beach and playground. A driving tour meanders to houses designed by local architect Earl Young. These fanciful dwellings, built with ice age stones and trademark wavy rooflines, look like hobbit houses.

**CRYSTAL MOUNTAIN RESORT & SPA** In Thompsonville (30 miles southwest of Traverse City), it has evolved into a first-class retreat. Whether guests come to ski, golf or hit the new Crystal Spa, they find ways to nourish mind, body and spirit. Lodgings range from hotel rooms to lovely three-bedroom cottages along the golf course and mountaintop homes where you can ski out your back door. Splashing in the enormous pool and water playground, mountain biking and golfing on two player-friendly courses entertain families who fill the resort in summer. You can find quiet along the forested trails that wind through 40-plus sculptures in the

Downtown Suttons Bay charms with a diverse mix of shops and cafes. *(Right)* A selection of fine hand-crafted wines produced from Chateau Chantal's vineyards on Old Mission Peninsula.

resort's Michigan Legacy Art Park. The spa soothes with organic decor and services like the fresh-air facial.

**GASLIGHT DISTRICT** Petoskey's century-old shopping district, sloping down to a Little Traverse Bay beach, has been ably entertaining vacationers since they arrived in old-time lake steamers. Overall, though, the shopping vibe is cutting-edge and creative. 52 Weekends seems to hold enough discoveries for a year—clothes and jewelry as well as fun serving pieces and decorations. A wide selection, including an exceptional regional section, packs two levels at McLean & Eakin Booksellers. Cutler's is a premier source for furnishing perfect lake cottages.

**THE HOMESTEAD** A Lake Michigan beach lures families to this retreat (25 miles northwest of Traverse City). Almost surrounded by vast Sleeping Bear Dunes National Lakeshore, the historic inn anchors more than 700 condos, hotel rooms and vacation homes.

**STUDIO AND GALLERIES** Artists flourish almost as surely as orchards and vineyards in this region. Our list of must-stops includes Bier Art Gallery, showing the works of 44 artists, including that of owners Ray and Tami Bier and their son, Tyler, in a converted red schoolhouse. We love funky, colorful pieces at Michigan Artists Gallery in Suttons Bay. Mullaly's 128 Gallery in Elk Rapids (north of Traverse City) features an irresistible jewelry collection. Also in Elk Rapids, the Twisted Fish Art Gallery showcases sculpture in a pretty garden and more pieces in two converted cottages.

**WEATHERVANE TERRACE INN & SUITES** This well-cared-for motel along the Pine River in Charlevoix qualifies as a genuine classic as well as a good value. Charlevoix architect Earl Young designed the lobby and its massive stone fireplace. Spacious rooms have been comfortably updated. Some suites have rowboat-size whirlpool tubs and balconies with views of Lake Michigan.

## FOUR FABULOUS PLATES

### Fresh Start @ Nonna's

At the Homestead Resort in Glen Arbor near Sleeping Bear Dunes National Lakeshore, the Zuppa d'Asparagi starts with asparagus from Michigan's Norconk Farms. This fresh-as-a-lake-breeze version adds toasted pine nuts and tomato bruschetta, which give the creamy soup a zingy citrusy kick and hearty chunky texture.

### Dinner @ Phil's on Front

Savor signature blue lump crab puffs in a sleek downtown Traverse City setting. Cap your meal with freshly made truffles from the case at the front of this restaurant and chocolate bar.

### Tasting @ Leelanau Cellars

Looking out on Lake Michigan in Onema, Leelanau Cellars' tasting room offers sips of an exceptional selection of vintages, including a lovely fruity Pinot Grigio and a dry Sleeping Bear Red.

### Bistro fare @ Cafe Sante

In Boyne City, watch the sunset along Lake Charlevoix over truffled wild mushroom wood-fired pizza or one of the pasta dishes made in-house and fresh daily. We had the melt-in-your-mouth cheese ravioli. Still hungry? Finish your meal off with homemade tiramisu or chocolate hazelnut cake.

A gorgeous sunrise view from Chateau Grand Traverse. *(Right)* Wine tasting at Chateau Chantal, one of several wineries on Old Mission Peninsula.

> "I've always lived and worked in areas known for their natural beauty; ... However, few places can rival northern Michigan's natural beauty combined with its rich agriculture. ... The rolling hills, punctuated by the farms, orchards and vineyards, make for scenery that is unrivaled."

— FRED LAUGHLIN, GREAT LAKES CULINARY INSTITUTE

PHOTOGRAPH: BOB STEFKO

Savor breathtaking views of Grand Traverse Bay from Chateau Chantal's vineyards on Old Mission Peninsula.

# CHERRY CHILI

*Staffers at Cherry Republic put the store's signature tangy fruit salsa to good use in this white-bean-chicken chili, which won the local chili competition. It's served in their restaurant with corn chips or their cherry-sage corn bread.*

Start to finish: 40 minutes

1 tablespoon butter
1½ cups finely chopped celery
1 cup finely chopped onion
1 cup finely chopped green sweet pepper
3 cloves garlic, minced
2 15- to 16-ounce cans great Northern or cannellini beans (white kidney beans), rinsed and drained
2 14-ounce cans chicken broth
1 9-ounce jar Cherry Republic Hot Cherry Salsa or 1 cup desired purchased salsa
3 cups cubed cooked chicken or turkey
2 teaspoons ground cumin
2 bay leaves
½ cup half-and-half or light cream
2 tablespoons cornstarch
Salt
Ground black pepper
Cherry Republic Hot Cherry Salsa or 1 cup desired purchased salsa (optional)
Sliced green onion (optional)

**1.** In a 4-quart Dutch oven, melt butter over medium heat. Add celery, onion, sweet pepper and garlic; cook until tender, stirring occasionally. Add the drained beans, broth, the 1 cup cherry salsa, chicken, cumin and bay leaves. Bring to boiling; reduce heat. Simmer, uncovered, for 10 minutes.
**2.** In a screw-top jar, combine half-and-half and cornstarch. Cover and shake well; stir into the chili. Cook and stir until slightly thickened and bubbly. Cook and stir for 2 minutes more. Season to taste.
**3.** To serve, remove and discard bay leaves. Ladle chili into bowls and top with additional salsa and green onion, if you like. **Makes 8 servings.**

## Cherries rule!

"It really is about making memories," says Bob Sutherland, owner of Cherry Republic. "When people open that box of chocolate-covered cherries, they recall this place." The Glen Arbor institution has been fueling vacationers' memories since 1988. Besides the main store, there's a bakery and cafe, a winery, and thriving mail-order and online businesses. Bob offers 174 cherry food products, many available for sampling, from trademark Boomchunka cookies (clerks beat a drum with every sale) to barbecue sauce and salad dressing. You even can buy chocolate-covered cherry pits!

Ingredients are easy to come by, as area growers harvest 175 million pounds a year, three-quarters of the national total. They also produce about 45 million pounds of sweet cherries, the kind that wind up brined as maraschinos or that you just pop into your mouth.

Fields of high-quality asparagus at Norconk Farm in Honor. (*Above*) Make entertaining easy with a brunch featuring asparagus scramble biscuits.

# ASPARAGUS SCRAMBLE BISCUITS

*An abundance of asparagus in Michigan leads to inspiring dishes. These alternative breakfast sandwiches' bacon biscuits can be made ahead of time. Then add fresh asparagus, vegetables and eggs for an impromptu brunch.*

Prep: 30 minutes  Bake: 5 minutes

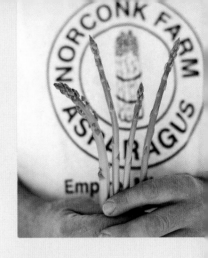

8 ounces fresh asparagus, trimmed and cut into bite-size pieces
1 tablespoon butter
12 eggs, lightly beaten
½ teaspoon salt
½ teaspoon cracked black pepper
¾ cup roasted red sweet peppers, chopped
  Bacon-Cheddar Cornmeal Biscuits (recipe follows)
¾ cup shredded Swiss cheese (3 ounces)

**1.** In a large skillet, cook asparagus in hot butter over medium heat about 6 minutes or until crisp-tender. Remove asparagus from skillet.
**2.** Add eggs, salt and black pepper to skillet. Using a spatula, lift and fold cooked egg, letting uncooked egg run underneath. Cook about 4 minutes or until almost set; stir in roasted peppers and asparagus. Remove from heat.
**3.** Split the Bacon-Cheddar Cornmeal Biscuits in half horizontally. Arrange bottoms of biscuits in a 15x10x1-inch baking pan. Divide egg mixture and Swiss cheese among biscuit bottoms. Add biscuit tops.
**4.** Bake, uncovered, in a 350° oven for 5 to 8 minutes or until heated through and cheese is melted. **Makes 8 (2-biscuit) servings.**

**Bacon-Cheddar Cornmeal Biscuits:** Stir together 1¾ cups all-purpose flour, ½ cup cornmeal and 1 tablespoon baking powder. Cut ¼ cup cold butter into flour mixture until butter is size of small peas. Add ¾ cup shredded cheddar cheese; 4 slices bacon, crisp-cooked, drained and crumbled; ²/₃ cup milk; 1 egg, lightly beaten; and 2 tablespoons snipped fresh chives. Stir just until moistened. Turn dough out onto a lightly floured surface. Knead by gently folding dough for four to six strokes. Pat into an 8-inch square that is ½ inch thick. Cut into sixteen 2-inch squares. Place squares 1 inch apart on a lightly greased baking sheet. Brush squares with additional milk. Bake in a 425° oven for 10 to 12 minutes or until golden brown. Remove from baking sheet. Cool on a wire rack. Makes 16 biscuits.

## Stalking fresh success

Asparagus thrives in well-drained, sandy soil and in a lake-tempered climate. Michigan grows a lot of the succulent, apple-green spears, mostly in Oceana County, along the Lake Michigan shore.

Harry Norconk, a pioneer of sorts, has 40 acres all told. His Jersey Knight and Jersey Giant asparagus plants have grown up to 8 feet tall, replenishing the root systems that will send up tender shoots for harvesting in May and June. The plants will be mowed down in November, and a freshly seeded crop of rye will flourish as a winter blanket over their heads.

Harry supplies almost half of his crop to local restaurants. He's so enthusiastic about his main crop that he instigated an annual asparagus festival, held each May in Empire, complete with an Ode to Asparagus poetry reading and an asparagus-throwing contest!

PHOTOGRAPHS: BOB STEFKO (OPPOSITE, FROM TOP) AND LYONS, BOB STEFKO

# OATMEAL CHERRY COOKIES

*Michigan produces about 175 million pounds of cherries each year, and the Traverse City area grows 75 percent of the country's tart cherries. This recipe from American Spoon Foods highlights the local fruit in delicious cookies.*

Prep: 30 minutes  Bake: 12 minutes per batch  Cool: 1 minute per batch

- 1 cup butter, softened
- 1 cup packed dark brown sugar
- ½ cup granulated sugar
- 1½ teaspoons baking powder
- 1 teaspoon ground cinnamon
- ½ teaspoon salt
- ½ teaspoon baking soda
- 2 eggs
- 1 teaspoon vanilla
- 2 cups all-purpose flour
- 2 cups rolled oats
- 1 cup snipped American Spoon Dried Red Tart Cherries or dried red cherries (6 ounces)

**1.** In a large mixing bowl, beat butter with an electric mixer on medium to high speed for 30 seconds. Add brown sugar, granulated sugar, baking powder, cinnamon, salt and baking soda. Beat until combined, scraping sides of bowl occasionally. Beat in eggs and vanilla until combined. Beat in as much of the flour as you can with the mixer. Using a wooden spoon, stir in the remaining flour. Stir in oats and dried cherries.

**2.** Drop the dough by rounded teaspoons 2 inches apart onto ungreased cookie sheets.

**3.** Bake in a 350° oven about 12 minutes or until the edges are lightly browned. Cool on cookie sheet for 1 minute. Transfer the cookies to a wire rack; cool. **Makes about 60 cookies.**

TIP: Butter adds flavor, richness and texture to cookies—substitute another ingredient only if the option is offered. Make sure the butter you use has softened to room temperature, about 30 minutes. It should have lost its chill and be spreadable. Never use melted butter unless the recipe calls for it.

## Eating fresh with a spoon

With seven Michigan stores including the Petoskey flagship, American Spoon Foods founder Justin Rashid has built a national following championing the flavors of Michigan's fields and forests.

Justin's father, a Lebanese-American grocer from the Detroit area, bought a northern Michigan farm as a summer getaway in the 1950s. Both of Justin's parents shared a passion for fresh, natural foods, so part of their fun was foraging for wild berries and fruits and selling them at a family summer produce stand.

In 1979, after Justin and his wife, Kate Marshall, settled in Petoskey, he began supplying morel mushrooms to a New York chef. Soon, the two forged a partnership that blossomed into American Spoon Foods.

"We're perched at the top of one of the most superb fruit-growing regions of the country," Justin says.

# CHUBBY MARY

*The Cove restaurant in the fishing town of Leland adds a local twist to its Bloody Mary. A 6-inch smoked fish stands upright in the drink. Prepare to be pleasantly surprised at the smoky flavor this innovative swizzle stick adds.*

Start to finish: 20 minutes

- 3 tablespoons lime or lemon juice (1½ ounces)
- 1 teaspoon prepared horseradish
- ⅛ teaspoon celery seeds
- 1 cup tomato juice, chilled (8 ounces)
- 1 teaspoon Worcestershire sauce
- ¼ to ½ teaspoon bottled hot pepper sauce
  Dash kosher salt or salt
  Dash freshly ground black pepper
- ¾ cup vodka, chilled in the freezer (6 ounces)
  Ice cubes
- 2 6-ounce whole smoked chubs, trout or whitefish
- 2 kosher dill pickles or cucumber spears
- 4 large pimento-stuffed green olives

**1.** For mix: In a small pitcher or 2-cup glass measure, combine lime juice, horseradish and celery seeds. Mash the mixture with the end of a wooden spoon to blend and break up the celery seeds. Pour in the tomato juice, Worcestershire sauce, hot sauce, salt and black pepper. Stir everything to combine.

**2.** To serve, divide the vodka between two tall, chilled glasses filled with ice cubes. Fill the glasses with the tomato juice mixture; stir.

**3.** For each serving, add a smoked chub and a kosher dill pickle to glass. Thread two of the olives on a cocktail pick; place across rim of glass. **Makes 2 (10-ounce) servings.**

**TIP:** If you don't have a juicer, use a fork. Insert the fork into cut fruit such as a lime or lemon. While gently squeezing the fruit, lift and lower fork to extract juice.

**TIP:** Because black pepper can lose flavor after it's ground, many cooks prefer to purchase whole peppercorns and grind them as needed. To do this, you need a pepper mill; most come with settings that allow coarse to finely ground pepper.

## What's brewing in the northwest?

Artisan ales are bubbling up in the region better known for vineyards and wineries.

Families love the burgers and lively atmosphere at Mackinaw Brewing Company, a downtown Traverse City fixture since 1997. North Peak Brewing Company, in a former candy factory, is a sweet addition to the Cherry Capital's brewpub scene. The cavernous building also houses a taste of Ireland at Kilkenny's Irish Public House. Need a haircut but want a beer? Head to the Warehouse District for both at Salon Saloon and Right Brain Brewery.

Old Mission Peninsula wineries have a new neighbor at Bowers Harbor, where Jolly Pumpkin Brewery serves rustic craft beers at the complex that includes the Mission Table restaurant. You'll find ales, not awls, at the hardware store that's now Short's Brewing Company in Bellaire.

## Southwest Road to Bounty

ALONG THE RED ARROW HIGHWAY, named for a WWI Army unit, clapboard cottages, galleries and antiques shops mingle with spots that qualify as gustatory shrines (the classic first-night vacation dinner has to be Redamaks in New Buffalo). But amid these classics, chefs seem to be working everywhere.

Inland, the region's dozen vineyards are creating notable wines, and one is even crafting vodka.

### TASTES GUIDE

Blossoms bursting forth on the trees of area orchards usher in the season. Visitors take breaks from the beaches and shore towns to make forays to inland fruit farms and vineyards. Just across the state line, New Buffalo has a nice downtown, a harbor and a boardwalk. Boutiques and restaurants dot the streets. As you follow the Red Arrow Highway north, Union Pier is

> **When I was an apprentice in Vienna, Austria, I read a book about the Great Lakes and how many states the lakes border, including Michigan. I strangely felt drawn to live in the area. I kept thinking,** *Wouldn't it be great to live in Michigan?*
>
> — HERMANN SUHS, HERMANN'S

the first of a string of lakeside resort towns, each with a tasty stop or two. St. Joseph, with a pretty downtown on a bluff above a Lake Michigan beach, serves as a northern gateway and another base for exploring this region. North of St. Joseph, South Haven, Saugatuck and Grand Haven swell into a summer-long party, with miles of appealing beaches walking distance from vibrant downtowns. You'll find classic as well as cutting-edge eateries, drawing on the best of local bounty and serving regional wines. For links and more details, visit michigan.org

**BREWSTER'S** In New Buffalo, the oddly Anglo name doesn't impact the authentic flavors at this Italian cafe. The decor is authentic, down to the fresco-esque painted walls and faux vines. Ditch the menu and go right for the pizza. Cooked in a wood-fired oven, it's cracker-crust thin but chewy. Try it topped with delicate artichokes and bits of ham.

**CONTESSA WINE CELLARS** You could mistake the tasting facility for a new home, if not for the signs. Notable wines include a semidry rosé called Prediletto Blush and a white variety called Chardonel. Down the road from Contessa, you'll make two more discoveries: The Chocolate Garden, a storybook-looking farmhouse shop where handmade truffles are sold, and Grandpa's Cider Mill with homemade cider and doughnuts.

**DOMAINE BERRIEN CELLARS** In Berrien Springs, this quality-conscious operation opened in 2001 with 21 varieties of wine grapes grown on 32 acres. Drive down its long entrance road, flanked by vines, to the small, nicely appointed tasting room. This is truly handmade wine, with 4,500 cases bottled manually each year. Dry wines are favored here, with a few sweet varieties, including a Cabernet Franc ice wine that has 22 percent residual sugar and a higher-than-normal alcohol content of 8.6 percent.

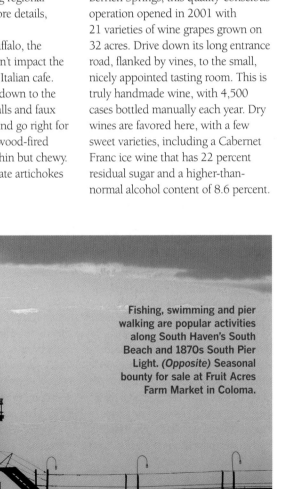

Fishing, swimming and pier walking are popular activities along South Haven's South Beach and 1870s South Pier Light. *(Opposite)* Seasonal bounty for sale at Fruit Acres Farm Market in Coloma.

## FIVE FABULOUS PLATES

### Breakfast@Rosie's Diner
The menu doesn't drift far from the staples at this New Buffalo diner. Plan on plenty of eggs, hash browns, pancakes, biscuits and gravy and coffee served in small white ceramic cups. This is where the locals eat, and people will tell you there's no more delicious or friendlier place to start the morning.

### Lunch@ Bentwood Tavern
New Buffalo's only waterfront restaurant is the place for admiring a marina full of gleaming cabin cruisers over garlicky shrimp and polenta.

### Apps@Timothy's
The creation of another Chicago transplant, this eatery's terra-cotta dining room is warm and contemporary. Start with crab cakes, not exactly a Michigan delicacy, but superb—tiny, perfectly crusted and flaky.

### Dinner@Skip's
The steak is rare, juicy and intense. The aggressive menu is not for the faint of heart—you actually can order a 42-ounce prime rib.

### Sweets@Oink's
You have to partake of this pastel theme park for dessert and pig lovers. It's jammed with stuff—not just pig memorabilia, but old signs, soda bottles, dolls, kites, toy animals and even vintage shoes. Oh, they serve ice cream, too.

*(From left)* Lush vineyards south of Lawton. In Baroda, Round Barn Winery's iconic turn-of-the-century Amish barn.

**FENN VALLEY VINEYARDS** Northwest of Paw Paw near Fennville, this award-winning winery makes impressive dry Riesling, a dry rosé called Desert Sunset, a late-harvest white Vignoles and Meritage, a traditional Bordeaux-style red.

**KARMA VISTA VINEYARDS & WINERY** Northwest of Coloma, this hilltop winery's name is "part metaphysical, part Madison Avenue," says owner Joe Herman. Try the Coloma Clearwater Riesling, with a distinct apple flavor and the dry red Stone Temple Pinot.

**LEMON CREEK WINERY** Part of a farm that's been in the Lemon family for 156 years, this operation has been known almost as long for its Kerner dry white (similar to a Johannisberg Riesling) in a traditional blue bottle. It was the first winery to plant Cabernet Sauvignon in Michigan, and offers a Cabernet ice wine, harvested midwinter.

**MILDA'S CORNER MARKET** This Lithuanian deli in Union Pier has a cult following—and a devoted Facebook page—for good reason. Everything in the tidy, red-painted store looks delicious, especially the *kugelis*—a casserole creation of onion, bacon, eggs, potatoes and milk.

**PHOENIX STREET CAFE** Voted as having the best breakfast in South Haven in recent years, this eatery holds an unassuming spot in the heart of the downtown shopping district. The dining room offers spare, clean decorating heavy on earth tones and vintage Chicago-area tourism posters. Several "best breakfast" joints in the area don't venture beyond pancakes, eggs and basic omelettes. The Phoenix adds more interesting choices such as eggs Benedict Florentine (with spinach and artichoke hearts) and bagels with salmon, lox, capers and

fresh veggies. The home fries are noteworthy on their own for a peppy dash of fresh herbs. Be sure to check the chalkboard for the daily breakfast and lunch specials.

**ROUND BARN WINERY** With two vintage barns and pretty grounds that are the setting for dozens of weddings each year, this distillery and brewery makes fruit brandies (apricot, Asian pear, black cherry, plum and others), cordials such as black walnut and elderberry, dessert wines and DiVine brand vodka. The 1911 round barn houses a restaurant and tasting bar.

**SALT OF THE EARTH** Lovers of fresh, local produce flock to this Fennville gem. The restaurant also purchases local cheeses, and cures, smokes and carves its own meats. You'll find a large selection of local beers and wines. A bakery sells desserts and crusty artisan breads.

(*From left*) Juicy black raspberries from Frank Farms in Berrien Center. Local growers at New Buffalo's Farmers Market.

Amid these classics, chefs seem to be working everywhere. Inland, the region's dozen vineyards craft notable wines. Towns that serve surrounding orchards, wineries and farms nurture rich food scenes of their own.

Be sure to check the Fresh Board for the evening's specials, usually related to seasonal produce. On a recent visit, fresh wild mushrooms inspired a savory and delicious ravioli and, for dessert, local blueberries starred in a sundae with white chocolate fudge, Tahitian vanilla gelato and honey.

**ST. JULIAN WINERY** Enjoy the scenery on the drive east to Paw Paw, with a historic courthouse and a downtown that looks like a movie set. The small town is one of the state's top destinations for wine lovers. Located here since 1936, St. Julian makes 40-plus varieties, including many award-winners, and offers free tours and tastings.

**WARNER VINEYARDS** Another of the state's largest wineries, in Paw Paw next door to St. Julian, the handsome brick building dates to 1898. At Michigan's second oldest winery, still family owned, learn how champagne is made on a self-guided tour that includes the cool (literally) aging European caves.

**BETWEEN MEALS**

**HARBOR GRAND** A real benefit of staying at this 55-room boutique hotel is the relatively higher level of personal service. As a guest here, you'll get complimentary breakfast delivered to your room. You can take advantage of the hotel's 24-hour Ben & Jerry's ice cream delivery. Guests also can use beach bikes, beach towels and sand chairs—for free.

Another hotel amenity we love is the professionally staffed massage center (reservations recommended).

**NEW BUFFALO CITY BEACH** Great sand is easy to come by in southwestern Michigan, but New Buffalo's stands out. The parking lot connects to a boardwalk that takes you past a playground and to the water's edge where lifeguards are on duty. The town lighthouse stands just to the left, and dune grasses provide a backdrop.

PHOTOGRAPH: KEVIN I MIYAZAKI/REDUX

> "While at culinary school in New York, I was introduced to the fact that southwest Michigan is such a bountiful area. It took moving away to realize how amazing this area is."
>
> — JOHN PAUL VERHAGE, TABOR HILL

Beach time along Lake Michigan at the new Jean Klock Park in Benton Harbor. (*Opposite*) Joe Herman inspects his Karma Vista Vineyards in Coloma.

# BLUEBERRY CREAM TREATS

*When it's time for the blueberry harvest at DeGrandchamp Farms in South Haven, this quick dessert fits their busy schedule. It's so simple, yet so good.*

Start to finish: 10 minutes

~~~~~~~~~~~~~~~~~~~~~~~~~~~~~~~~~~~~~~~~~~~~~~~~

- 1   8-ounce carton dairy sour cream
- ¼   cup packed brown sugar
- 1   quart (4 cups) fresh blueberries
     Brown sugar (optional)

**1.** In a small bowl, stir together the sour cream and the ¼ cup brown sugar until a smooth cream forms.
**2.** To serve, divide blueberries among six stemmed sherbet dishes or dessert dishes. Spoon sour cream mixture over blueberries. If you like, sprinkle with additional brown sugar.
**Makes 6 servings.**

**Blueberry-Banana Smoothie:** In a blender, combine a 6-ounce carton of blueberry yogurt, ½ cup orange juice, half of a ripe banana, ½ cup fresh or frozen blueberries, 2 tablespoons honey and 1 cup small ice cubes or crushed ice. Cover and blend until nearly smooth. Makes 2 servings.

**Blueberry Milk Shake:** In a blender, combine 1 pint vanilla ice cream, 2 cups fresh or frozen blueberries and ½ to ¾ cup milk. Cover and blend until smooth. Makes 2 servings.

**TIP:** Turn ordinary muffins into extraordinary treats by adding a scoop of blueberries to the batter. To keep the juicy berries from turning the batter blue, use whole blueberries when possible. When using canned blueberries, drain well and carefully blot dry with paper towels. If you are using frozen blueberries, add them to the batter while still frozen. No matter what form you use, gently stir the berries into the batter just before spooning it into the baking pans.

**TIP:** Blueberries are in season late May through October. To buy fresh blueberries, look for a dark blue color with a soft powdery bloom. Blueberry size is an indication of quality; large and plump blueberries are deemed most desirable. Blueberries are perishable and should be used soon after purchase. Store berries loosely covered in the refrigerator for 10 to 14 days and wash just before use.

## South Haven: It's the berries!

Summer belongs to blueberries in the four counties around South Haven along Lake Michigan and the southwest Michigan shore. In fact, this region ranks first in the nation for cultivating these little blue gems.

You can time your visit for the Blueberry Festival in August. Roadside stands sell fresh fruit, jams and pies. Or, you can head for you-pick farms, most with fruit markets. DeGrandchamp's, Jones, LeDuc, Stephenson Farms, True Blue and The Berry Patch are popular berry farms.

In South Haven's lively downtown, the Blueberry Store stocks everything blueberry, from teas and preserves to blueberry-themed china.

Restaurants throughout the area feature blueberry specialties in season. The homespun restaurant at Crane's Pie Pantry in nearby Fennville features legendary blueberry pie.

PHOTOGRAPHS: KEVIN J. MIRAGAVA/BLOOM (OR PURELY) RUBEN JACOBS

Try warm apple spice crumble for a no-fuss dessert. *(Below, from left)* Peaches, apricots, apples—you can pick your own at Tree-Mendus Fruit farm in Eau Claire. Apple picking is a family affair at Witte Orchards in Dimondale.

# WARM APPLE SPICE CRUMBLE

*This easy, homey treat lets you bring a fresh-baked warm dessert to the table in less than half an hour. Canned sliced apples and purchased granola make it easy to assemble.*

Prep: 15 minutes  Bake: 12 minutes

1 20-ounce can sliced apples
¼ cup golden raisins or mixed dried fruit bits
1 teaspoon vanilla
2 to 3 tablespoons sugar
1 teaspoon Apple Pie Spice (recipe follows)
    or ground cinnamon
3 tablespoons butter, cut into small pieces
1½ cups low-fat granola
¼ cup flaked coconut
    Vanilla ice cream (optional)

**1.** In a 8x8-inch baking dish (2-quart square), combine the undrained apples and raisins. Stir in vanilla. Sprinkle sugar and Apple Pie Spice over apples. Top with butter pieces. Sprinkle granola and coconut evenly over apple mixture.
**2.** Bake in a 375° oven for 12 to 15 minutes or until apples are heated through and topping is golden brown. Serve warm with vanilla ice cream, if you like. **Makes 4 servings.**

**Apple Pie Spice:** Combine ½ teaspoon ground cinnamon, ¼ teaspoon ground nutmeg, ⅛ teaspoon ground allspice, and a dash ground cloves or ground ginger. Makes 1 teaspoon.

**Apple varieties:** Commercial growers produce about 300 varieties of apples, although there are 2,500 varieties grown in the United States.

**How to store:** Store apples in a refrigerator for up to 6 weeks; store bulk apples in a cool, moist place. Keeping apples at room temperature causes them to lose crispness and flavor and to ripen about 10 times faster.

TIP: Once cut, apples brown easily. Sprinkle apple pieces and slices with lemon, orange or grapefruit juice mixed with water, or treat them with ascorbic acid color keeper.

## Michigan's big apple

Tree-Mendus Fruit farm lives up to its name in Eau Claire. The 450-acre, family-owned orchard nurtures more than 200 varieties of apples. It's one of the largest of a dozen-plus fruit farms that flourish in the lake-tempered climate.

Visitors can pick their own or grab a peck near the store entrance. There's lots of open space and even a playground where kids can run.

Patrons meander through the rows of trees to search for their favorite varieties. You'll find lesser-known apples like Pink Sparkle—firm, tart and colored with a sunburst of bubblegum pink inside. There are also plenty of popular standards, such as Jonathan, Fuji, Gala, Red Delicious and Honeycrisp.

"What's your favorite apple?" someone asks Gary Wesolowski manning the store's counter. "The next one," he says with a grin.

PHOTOGRAPHS: KEVIN J. MIYAZAKI/REDUX. (OPPOSITE, CLOCKWISE FROM TOP) MARK THOMAS, TODD ZAWISTOWSKI, KEVIN J. MIYAZAKI/REDUX

# AHI TUNA

*"In this light, summertime dish," explains chef John Paul Verhage, "I make the most of fresh tuna and fruit." Ahi, with its mild, meaty flavor, tastes exceptional with a pineapple sauce zinged with ginger, papaya-studded rice and citrusy Tabor Hill Barrel Select Chardonnay.*

Prep: 30 minutes  Marinate: 30 minutes  Cook: 45 minutes  Grill: 6 minutes

~~~~~~~~~~~~~~~~~~~~~~~~~~~~~~~~~~~~~~~~~~~~

|   |   |
|---|---|
| 4 | 6- to 7-ounce fresh or frozen Ahi tuna steaks, cut 1 inch thick |
| ½ | cup soy sauce |
| 2 | tablespoons orange marmalade |
| 3 | cups unsweetened pineapple juice |
| 1 | tablespoon sugar |
| 1 | tablespoon grated fresh ginger |
| 1 | tablespoon lime juice |
| ⅛ | teaspoon crushed red pepper |
| 4 | ½-inch slices peeled and cored fresh pineapple |
|   | Jasmine Rice and Papaya (see recipe, page 148) |
| 1 | large ripe papaya, peeled, seeded and finely chopped |
|   | Green onions, trimmed and cut lengthwise into very thin strips |

**1.** Thaw tuna, if frozen. Rinse tuna; pat dry. Place tuna in a resealable plastic bag set in a shallow dish. For marinade: Combine soy sauce and marmalade. Pour marinade over tuna. Seal bag; turn to coat tuna. Marinate in the refrigerator for 30 minutes. Drain tuna, discarding marinade.
**2.** For pineapple sauce: Combine pineapple juice, sugar, ginger, lime juice and red pepper. Bring to boiling; reduce heat. Simmer, uncovered, until mixture is reduced to 1 cup, stirring occasionally. (Watch closely the last 10 minutes.)
**3.** For a charcoal grill: Place tuna and pineapple slices on the greased rack of an uncovered grill directly over medium coals. Grill for 6 to 7 minutes or just until tuna starts to flake when tested with a fork but center is still pink and pineapple is heated through, turning tuna and pineapple once halfway through grilling. (For a gas grill: Preheat grill. Reduce heat to medium. Place tuna and pineapple on greased grill rack over heat. Cover and grill as above.) Remove from grill. Let tuna stand for 1 to 2 minutes before slicing.
**4.** For each serving, place a pineapple slice on plate. Mound the Jasmine Rice and Papaya on top of pineapple. Place tuna around rice. Drizzle with pineapple sauce. Garnish with papaya and green onion strips. **Makes 4 servings.**

PHOTOGRAPHS: KEVIN J. MIYAZAKI/REDUX

## Vintage fine dining

The same devotion to quality that produces Tabor Hill's wines goes into creating culinary masterpieces for the winery's acclaimed restaurant. Menus are always based on the best and freshest ingredients available locally.

In addition to innovations like the tuna (*above*), the menu features favorites that include crab cakes with cherry wine sauce, a starter that's exceptionally good with another of the restaurant's signature dishes: cream of asparagus, Parmesan and Vidalia onion soup. A local grower and the farmers market supply most of the vegetables.

The restaurant's view is almost as stunning as the food. Diners gaze out of soaring, two-story windows over a rolling landscape of Chardonnay grapevines— even prettier bathed in soft sunset light.

A surprise ingredient tames three-alarm chili. *(Below, from left)* Sidewalk dining at New Holland Brewing Company. Drawing a beer at Jamesport Brewing Company in Ludington.

# THREE-ALARM LANSING FIRE CHILI

*No one knows hot like the local fire department. However, Lansing Fire Department's Matt Holzhei's chili generates just the right amount of tasty heat. A surprise ingredient—a chocolate bar—gets credit for the mellower flavor.*

Prep: 25 minutes  Roast: 2½ hours  Cook: 2 hours  Stand: 45 minutes

|   |   |
|---|---|
| 1 | 1- to 1½-pounds boneless beef chuck pot roast |
| 1¼ | cups water |
| 3 | beef bouillon cubes or 3 teaspoons instant beef bouillon granules |
| 2 | 28-ounce cans diced tomatoes |
| 1 | large onion, chopped |
| 1 | green sweet pepper, chopped |
| 1 | red sweet pepper, chopped |
| 1 | fresh jalapeño chile pepper, seeded and chopped |
| 1 | tablespoon hot chili powder |
| 3 | cloves garlic, minced |
| 1½ | teaspoons ground cumin |
| 8 | ounces bulk hot Italian sausage |
| ½ | of a 6-ounce milk chocolate or dark chocolate candy bar, cut up |
| 1 | cup fresh, frozen or drained canned whole kernel corn |
| 2 | 22- to 30-ounce cans chili beans with chili gravy |
|   | Shredded cheddar cheese |
|   | Corn chips (optional) |

**1.** Trim fat from meat. In a 6-quart oven-safe Dutch oven, combine the meat, the water and bouillon. Roast, covered, in a 350° oven for 2½ to 3 hours or until the meat is very tender. Remove meat from the Dutch oven; let stand for 30 minutes. Reserve ¼ cup of the beef drippings.

**2.** In the same Dutch oven, combine the reserved ¼ cup beef drippings, the undrained tomatoes, onion, green and red sweet peppers, jalapeño, hot chili powder, garlic and cumin. Bring to boiling; reduce heat. Simmer, covered, for 1 hour, stirring occasionally.

**3.** Meanwhile, shred meat by pulling two forks through it in opposite directions to gently separate the meat into long thin strands. Cover and chill meat until needed.

*Continued on page 144*

## What's brewing in the southwest?

Wine gets more buzz. But almost 20 microbreweries and brewpubs have built loyal followings. Some highlights:

• Bell's Brewery of Kalamazoo became the first Michigan brewery to serve beer by the glass to the public on June 11, 1993. The Eccentric Cafe offers customers tastes of well-known beers as well as small-batch brews.

• New Holland Brewing Company started in Holland in 1997 as a two-man operation. Now, two locations brew and serve seasonal specialties such as Golden Cap for summer and Cabin Fever in winter.

• Old Boys' Brewhouse, founded in 1997 in Spring Lake by three partners and named after Old Boy, a chocolate Lab, produces hand-crafted ales using the freshest ingredients.

• Saugatuck Brewing Company, a microbrewery and its Irish-style Lucky Stone Pub, create and serve 11 unique brews.

PHOTOGRAPHS: JOHN NOLTNER (OPPOSITE, CLOCKWISE FROM TOP) ROBERT JACOBS, JOHN NOLTNER (2)

With more than 250 vendors and merchants, Detroit's Eastern Market draws tens of thousands to its Saturday market. *(Opposite)* Rows of fresh and seasonal produce.

PHOTOGRAPHS: KEVIN J. MIYAZAKI/REDUX

# Meandering the Artful Southeast Trail

LOOK BEYOND DETROIT and its iconic Eastern Market and downtown restaurants to communities that ring the city. Surrounded by some of the state's richest farmland and brimming with discriminating diners, these towns act like incubators, nurturing innovative chefs and fledgling flavors. This ever-rich food scene is reaching north to the tip of the Thumb and fanning west and south.

## TASTES GUIDE

Except for UM game weekends and Ann Arbor's iconic art festivals running simultaneously in July, this region is a great place to leave the city behind and immerse yourself in small-town charm. For more ideas and links, visit michigan.org.

ANN ARBOR Adjacent to iconic Zingerman's (see page 89) in the University of Michigan's lively hometown, Ann Arbor Farmers Market has one of the biggest gatherings of fresh, local foods in southeast Michigan. Chefs revere this extravaganza of heirloom tomatoes, baby lettuce and other artisan vegetables. The market also is well laid-out, visually appealing, and loaded with samples like vegan brownies, housemade mozzarella and poppy seed baguettes.

Next door in a repurposed building, Kerrytown Market & Shops houses its own culinary treasures. Sparrow Market has all manner of free-range meat and poultry, while Durham's claims to "smoke salmon before your very eyes." In the beverage arena, Everyday Wines "conspires to provide affordable wines." They specialize in offbeat pours like Vinho

## FIVE FABULOUS PLATES

### Brunch@Zola Cafe
At Ann Arbor's coolest downtown brunch spot, savor a perfectly fluffy omelet with asparagus and goat cheese.

### Lunch@Mediterrano
We love the griddled Halloumi cheese served with chili-roasted portobello and basil pesto, and Medjool dates wrapped in chorizo.

### Dinner@Zingerman's Roadhouse
Melt-in-your-mouth North Carolina pulled pork, seasoned by 14 hours over the coals—and a pinch of that good old Zingerman's magic—make this a required course in Ann Arbor. And don't pass up some of the menu's more standard-looking staples. Good old mac and cheese is anything but ordinary in the hands of these masters.

### Drinks@Eve
At this Kerrytown neighborhood restaurant, try an after-dinner martini with sugared mint leaves that seem to magically melt in your mouth.

### Utensil-free dining@ The Blue Nile
Just west of University of Michigan's campus, prepare to eat with your hands at this authentic restaurant, where you'll likely scoop up your food with a piece of spongy flatbread.

*(From left)* Farmer Dale Jenuwine at the Farmers Market. Wine barrels at Cherry Creek Vineyard & Winery in Cement City.

Verde, a Portuguese blend. At the People's Food Co-Op of Ann Arbor, the vibe is distinctly post-Woodstock. Walls of grains and loads of hemp are a throwback, but its Cafe Verde serves a mean smoked mozzarella frittata.

Before putting down roots in Ann Arbor and opening his cozy restaurant, Amadeus owner Paul Strozynski made stops in Austria and Chicago. Open since 1988, the cafe exudes old-world charm, from its ornate storefront to the paintings on the walls. Hearty fare peppers the menu where you'll find chicken paprikash, Hungarian goulash, kielbasa, pierogi and potato pancakes.

Tucked in the back of an office building, Silvio's family-owned restaurant looks like an unlikely spot for pizza. But the thin crust, organic ingredients and wood-burning oven are a match made in pizzeria heaven.

Since 1937, Weber's has been the place where Ann Arbor locals have gone for tasty American fare and personal service. Noted for its tender and savory prime rib and seafood, the restaurant also has a dessert selection sure to break your willpower. Save room for fresh strawberry shortcake that's everything it should be—tender, flaky and topped with juicy berries.

**MOUNT CLEMENS** In this waterfront town north of Detroit, the 30-year-old farmers market hosts many local farms, notably Gass Centennial Farm, the granddaddy of them all. Owned by innovative farmers Ellen and Bill Gass, the farm produces, for starters, 50 kinds of heirloom tomatoes, 60 kinds of lettuce and 10 kinds of herbs. Postmarket, head next door to Captain's Landing, a boat-cum-restaurant on the Clinton River. Try the whitefish and enjoy the nautical vibe,

down to the buoys and varnished wood. Baskets of red geraniums and daisies flank tables under umbrellas on the dock. Down the road along the waterfront, Crews Inn has boat slips in front. Sit outside, marvel at the boats and munch signature smelt—minnow-size fried fish.

**SOUTHEAST WINE TRAIL** Vineyards and vintners are flourishing along the state's newest wine trail that travels two-lane highways twisting through the region known as the Irish Hills, southwest of Detroit. Pretty downtown Tecumseh claims Pentamere Winery in a brick 1871 building that housed a grocery, clothing store and diner in past lives. Notable wines made in the basement include Harvest Apple, a blend of eight apple varieties and hints of spice, a gingery Gewürztraminer and a peppery Cabernet Franc. Homesick

PHOTOGRAPHS: KEVIN J. MIYAZAKI/REDUX

*(From left)* A casual welcome at The Captain's Landing Restaurant in Mount Clemens. In Ann Arbor, one of Gratzi's artful entrees.

Look beyond Detroit and its iconic Eastern Market and downtown restaurants to communities that ring the city. Surrounded by some of the state's richest farmland, these towns nurture innovative chefs and fledgling flavors.

Brits can stroll across the street to the British Tea Garden to stock up on English staples or have a proper cup of tea. Don't miss the fresh goat and cow's milk cheeses made at Boulevard Market. Be sure to make a reservation at Evans Street Station to cap off a day of winery visiting. This destination restaurant has extraordinary food, much of it local.

To the west, along scenic US-12, once the main route between Detroit and Chicago, is Cherry Creek Vineyard & Winery, which opened in 2006 in an 1870 one-room schoolhouse. Try the farmhouse hard cider in half-gallon glass growlers and the tart cherry wine made with a Hungarian variety called Balaton. The reds are notable, too, including a Cabernet Sauvignon called Enigma and a Cabernet and Pinot Noir Proprietors Reserve blend.

In Jackson, Lone Oak Vineyard Estate and Sandhill Crane Vineyards flank I-94. Lone Oak is a working vineyard, with a strictly utilitarian tasting room, but it's producing some intriguing wines from Kip Barber, a vintner who thinks outside the box. Try the Vin Du Roi, a classic Bordeaux blend of estate-grown Cabernet Sauvignon, Cabernet Franc, Merlot and Petit Verdot. The Fleur Blanche, a blend of Vignoles and Seyval Blanc grapes, is a pleasing semidry white.

At Sandhill, a friendly Airedale named Rose greets visitors. She's pictured on the label of the Sassy Rosé bottled here. The winery, set amid grapevines, is known for its Vignoles, a dry white made from a French hybrid grape and semidry Traminette, an offshoot of a Gewürztraminer that has both pleasing fruit and floral notes. St. Julian, the state's largest winery based in Paw Paw in the southwest, also has a tasting room on I-94.

PHOTOGRAPHS: (FROM LEFT) KEVIN J. MIYAZAKI/REDUX, JOHN NOLTNER

PHOTOGRAPH: KEVIN J. MIYAZAKI/REDUX

Just north of Port Hope, the 1857 Pointe aux Barques Lighthouse is the oldest continuously operating one on the Great Lakes. *(Right, from top)* Classic pumpkin pie. Pick the perfect pumpkin from area growers. *(Previous spread)* Zingerman's Deli crafts legendary sandwiches.

# MOMMY'S PUMPKIN PIE

*Linda Hundt, owner of Sweetie-licious Bakery Cafe in Dewitt, created her pumpkin pie recipe from her mother's classic version. Cream and orange zest make for a dark mahogany pumpkin pie with traditional ginger-cinnamon-clove spiciness.*

Prep: 30 minutes  Bake: 1 hour  Cool: 1 hour

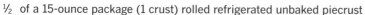

½  of a 15-ounce package (1 crust) rolled refrigerated unbaked piecrust
1  15-ounce can pumpkin
¾  cup packed brown sugar
1¼  teaspoons ground cinnamon
1  teaspoon ground ginger
½  teaspoon salt
¼  teaspoon ground cloves
¼  teaspoon finely shredded orange peel
4  eggs, lightly beaten
1½  cups half-and-half or light cream
   Whipped cream
   Granulated sugar
   Ground cinnamon

**1.** Let piecrust stand according to package directions. Unroll piecrust; place into a 9-inch pie plate. Tuck piecrust under and flute edges high. Do not prick piecrust. Line the piecrust with a double thickness of foil; add pie weights, if you like. Bake in a 400° oven for 15 minutes to partially bake piecrust. Remove foil and pie weights.
**2.** For filling: In a large bowl, stir together the pumpkin, brown sugar, the 1¼ teaspoons cinnamon, the ginger, salt, cloves and orange peel. Add eggs; beat lightly with a fork just until combined. Gradually add half-and-half;

stir until combined.
**3.** Place partially baked piecrust on the oven rack. Carefully pour filling into the piecrust-lined pie plate. To prevent overbrowning, cover edge of the pie with foil.
**4.** Bake in a 400° oven for 20 minutes. Remove the foil. Bake for 25 to 30 minutes more or until a knife inserted near the center comes out clean. Cool on a wire rack. Cover and store in the refrigerator within 2 hours. Serve pie with whipped cream lightly sprinkled with granulated sugar and additional cinnamon. **Makes 8 servings.**

## Michigan's green Thumb

Catch a greased pig, and you win the cheers and applause of the big crowd that gathers every summer for the Farmers Festival in Pigeon in the heart of the region north of Detroit known as the Thumb.

The summer celebration is among several that attract visitors to Michigan's most productive farm country. In the shadow of Cooperative Elevator Company's grain elevator, the state's largest, you can watch kiddie tractor pulls, stage performances, a parade and fireworks as well as eat tangy barbecue.

Most of the Thumb's interior pays tribute to the region's fertile soil. Sanilac County alone boasts more than 400 dairies. Two of the region's staple crops are beans and sugar beets. The annual Michigan Sugar Festival draws visitors to Sebewaing. Cotton candy spun from beet sugar is that event's star treat.

# FAMOUS BROWNIES

*These wallet-size brownies are one of the most popular sweets at Zingerman's Bakehouse in Ann Arbor. They bake about 1,000 each month. Manager Frank Carollo revealed the secret behind their great chocolate baked goods: Use the best ingredients.*

Prep: 25 minutes  Bake: 30 minutes

13   tablespoons butter
6½  ounces unsweetened chocolate, coarsely chopped
1½  cups sifted cake flour or all-purpose flour
¾   teaspoon baking powder
½   teaspoon salt
4   eggs
2   cups sugar
1¼  teaspoons vanilla
1¼  cups coarsely chopped walnuts, toasted

**1.** Grease a 13x9x2-inch baking pan; set aside. In a small heavy saucepan, heat the butter and chocolate over low heat, stirring constantly, until chocolate is melted and smooth. Set aside to cool. In a bowl, stir together the flour, baking powder and salt. Set aside.
**2.** In a large mixing bowl, beat eggs and sugar with an electric mixer on high speed about 5 minutes or until lemon-colored and fluffy, scraping sides of bowl occasionally.
**3.** Add cooled chocolate mixture and vanilla to egg mixture. Beat on low speed until combined. Add flour mixture. Beat on low speed until combined, scraping sides of bowl. Using a wooden spoon, stir in walnuts.
**4.** Spread batter in the prepared pan. Bake in a 325° oven about 30 minutes or until brownies appear set. Cool in pan on a wire rack. Cut into bars.
**Makes 15 brownies.**

**TIP:** Chocolate substitution. Although it's always best to use the type of chocolate called for in a recipe, in an emergency you can substitute 3 tablespoons unsweetened cocoa powder plus 1 tablespoon shortening or cooking oil for 1 square (1 ounce) unsweetened chocolate.

**TIP:** To avoid scorching chocolate when melting, use a heavy saucepan over low heat or a double boiler. This is no time to multitask! Watch carefully; stir often.

## Ann Arbor's foodie shrine

Everyone who visits the University of Michigan's hometown has to pay homage to Zingerman's Deli, even though it doesn't look like much of a culinary icon.

Opened in 1982 by Paul Saginaw and Ari Weinzweig near the farmers market, the tiny, redbrick storefront on Detroit Street stands off the college students' beaten path. A black awning with white writing and a big colorful sign in the window are the only clues to what's inside. The interior is small but stuffed with wonderful things—artisan breads, cheese and more than 30 kinds of olive oil.

Over almost three decades, the Zingerman family has grown to seven businesses, including Zingerman's Creamery, which makes the cheeses; Zingerman's Bakehouse, which crafts the breads; and Zingerman's Roadhouse, a laid-back eatery famous for its mac and cheese.

PHOTOGRAPHS: KEVIN J. MIYAZAKI/REDUX. (OPPOSITE) BOB STEFKO

The attractive business district in Northville, a Detroit suburb.
(*Above, from left*) Manning a booth at Detroit's Eastern Market.
Wilted spinach salad, a favorite at Cheli's Chili Bar in Dearborn.

# WILTED SPINACH SALAD

*Hockey fans love Cheli's Chili Bar in Dearborn. It's owned by the Red Wings' star hockey defenseman, Chris Chelios. Here's its delicious take on a classic side-dish salad.*

Start to finish: 25 minutes

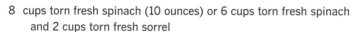

 8  cups torn fresh spinach (10 ounces) or 6 cups torn fresh spinach and 2 cups torn fresh sorrel
1½  cups sliced fresh mushrooms
 5  slices bacon, cut into 1-inch pieces
 ½  cup chopped onion, finely sliced leek or green onion
 2  cloves garlic, minced
 ¼  cup white vinegar
 1  tablespoon sugar
 ½  teaspoon instant beef bouillon granules
 ¼  teaspoon freshly ground black pepper
 1  hard-cooked egg, chopped

**1.** For salad: In a large salad bowl, toss together the spinach and mushrooms; set aside.
**2.** For dressing: In a very large skillet, cook bacon over medium heat until crisp, turning occasionally. Using a slotted spoon, remove bacon, reserving 2 tablespoons drippings in skillet (add olive oil, if necessary to measure 2 tablespoons). Drain the bacon on paper towels; crumble and set aside.
**3.** Add chopped onion and garlic to the 2 tablespoons reserved drippings. Cook and stir over medium-low heat until tender but not brown. Stir vinegar, sugar, bouillon granules and pepper into the drippings. Bring to boiling; remove from heat. Add the spinach mixture. Toss mixture in the skillet for 30 to 60 seconds or until spinach just starts to wilt.
**4.** Transfer mixture to the salad bowl or to individual salad plates. Sprinkle with bacon and chopped egg. Serve immediately. **Makes 4 to 6 servings.**

**TIP:** Store washed and dried greens in the refrigerator in a resealable plastic bag lined with paper towels or in a fabric produce bag. Spinach keeps about three days using this method.

**TIP:** For minced garlic, remove the cloves from the head. Peel away the papery skin and finely mince with a sharp knife or use a garlic press.

## What's brewing in the southeast?

You can hoist a glass at more than two dozen microbreweries and brewpubs in Detroit and the surrounding region. Some highlights:

• Atwater Block Brewery in Detroit uses a 200-year-old brewing process and brewing equipment from Germany. A shuttle runs to sporting events.

• Fort Street Brewery in Lincoln Park features a rotating selection of at least seven beers, with a new beer released every week. Tours are available weekday afternoons, evenings and Saturdays by appointment.

• Blue Tractor BBQ & Brewery in Ann Arbor has a concrete bar with a built-in ice rail to keep drinks cold. The brewers specialize in hoppy, astringent lagers and pilsners. A mix of bourbons and craft-brewed beers crown the drink menu, although retro beer like Pabst and Schlitz are sold.

Cherry pie—a Michigan tradition for good reason: The state produces 75 percent of the nation's tart cherries. For recipe, see page 152. *(Opposite)* A sweet treat from Tom's Mom's Cookies in Harbor Springs.

# {PURE} Tradition

Food fuels Michigan's vacation heritage. Take the ferry to historic Mackinac Island, and eat the best fudge on the planet. Hike, bike, hunt or snowmobile the Upper Peninsula, and dine on hearty pasties and woodland morels. Michigan shore? Blueberry pancakes and cherry pie. Huron shore? Whitefish and walleye—grilled, fried or tucked in a bun. Try these recipes when you need some of that spirit at home.

The massive exhibition halls of The Henry Ford capture the utility and glamour of the automobile in American life.

## An Automotive Legacy in Detroit and Beyond

HENRY FORD didn't invent the automobile. He transformed the world with plenty of help. In a burst of creative energy at the same time as airplanes were first taking to the skies and electric lights began illuminating cities, Ford and his fellow mechanics, engineers, tinkerers and visionaries marshaled an army of workers drawn from the fields and forests of America and the farms and cities of Europe. Together they perfected the car, created efficient assembly lines and built Michigan into the industrial powerhouse of the planet.

Following the path of those trailblazers takes you to one-of-a-kind museums, mansions, classic-car shows, factories and racetracks.

No other place distills Michigan's automotive heritage more richly than The Henry Ford in Dearborn, a western Detroit suburb and Ford's hometown. One of the world's largest museums, the complex includes Greenfield Village, a re-created turn-of-the-20th-century town. Greenfield Village houses hundreds of cars, as well as steam engines, trains, airplanes and even a stainless-steel diner. Visitors take Model T tours along broad streets lined with historic buildings, including the Wright Brothers' bicycle shop and Thomas Edison's laboratory.

Buses take visitors to Ford's massive historic River Rouge plant, where F-150 trucks now are assembled.

But you have to look farther than Dearborn for the complete picture. Lansing's R.E. Olds Transportation Museum tells the story of the Oldsmobile. In Flint, where General Motors was founded, the Alfred P. Sloan Museum showcases 25 classic Buicks.

If you visit in late August, make sure to take in the 16-mile parade of vintage cars purring through Detroit and its suburbs during the Woodward Dream Cruise. As you travel, don't be surprised if your memory cruises back to your first or favorite car. After all, you're in the land of automotive dreams.

*(Right)* Detail from a 1950s Ford El Dorado on display at The Henry Ford.

Henry Ford didn't invent the automobile. He transformed the world with plenty of help. No other place distills Michigan's automotive heritage more richly than The Henry Ford in Dearborn, a Detroit suburb.

## TASTES GUIDE

The auto empire throbs across Michigan's cities like a stroked-and-bored Flathead V8. Getting the whole story requires pilgrimages to where auto visionaries helped revolutionize transportation and to not-so-official car Meccas, where the pioneers' spirits live on. Classic restaurants and hotels will tide you over until your next trip.

**ANGELO'S CONEY ISLAND** A Flint landmark, the humble 1949 eatery (with a few satellite locations) is a shrine for lovers of the iconic hot dog smothered in meat sauce.

**BOMBER RESTAURANT** Huge portions are the hallmark of Ypsilanti's famous 65-year-old breakfast and lunch eatery that showcases photos, models and memorabilia honoring the World War II B-24 Liberator bombers built at Ford's Willow Run plant.

**CLARA'S LANSING STATION** Save room for a colossal slice of carrot cake at this Lansing favorite housed in the 1903 Michigan Central Railroad Depot. One look at the soaring ceiling, stained-glass windows and round turrets and it's easy to imagine the century-ago bustle of passengers.

**SOUP SPOON CAFE** The line is out the door at this tiny cafe (open for breakfast and lunch) about 1 mile from the R.E. Olds Transportation Museum in Lansing. Nick Gavrilides, the owner, works miracles in the small open kitchen using almost all Michigan ingredients.

## BETWEEN MEALS

**ALFRED P. SLOAN MUSEUM** General Motors was born in Flint. Sit behind the wheel of a 1917 touring car or at the 1940s soda fountain in the museum's Buick Automotive Gallery and Research Center.

**CROSSROADS VILLAGE & HUCKLEBERRY RAILROAD** After browsing the 35 shops and homes of this re-created turn-of-the-20th-century village near Flint, rest your feet three ways: ride the 1912 carousel, board the narrow-gauge steam train for a 40-minute ramble or cruise on the replica *Genesee Belle* paddle wheeler.

**DEARBORN INN** Built by Ford in 1931, this stately Georgian-style inn and spa (managed by Marriott) anchors 23 lush acres three blocks from The Henry Ford and Greenfield Village. Dine in two restaurants or the lounge.

**ENGLISH INN** The opulent 1927 Tudor Revival-style home of an Oldsmobile executive welcomes guests as a bed

PHOTOGRAPHS: BOB STEFKO

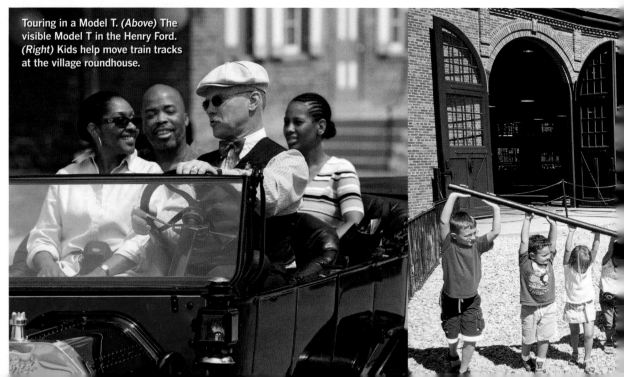

Touring in a Model T. *(Above)* The visible Model T in the Henry Ford. *(Right)* Kids help move train tracks at the village roundhouse.

and breakfast south of Lansing. The restaurant serves lunch and dinner.

**FORD PIQUETTE AVENUE PLANT** Ford's Model T was built in this redbrick building near downtown Detroit. View Fords in the bays where more than 12,000 were built in the early 1900s.

**FORD ROUGE FACTORY TOUR** Take a bus from The Henry Ford to watch F-150 trucks get assembled on the moving line at the Dearborn plant.

**GILMORE CAR MUSEUM** The collection in Hickory Corners (18 miles northeast of Kalamazoo) includes a London double-decker bus, more than 200 vehicles and a 1930s gas station. Lunch at the Blue Moon Diner.

**MICHIGAN HISTORICAL MUSEUM** In Lansing, the 31 permanent galleries include a re-creation of the 1957 Detroit Auto Show complete with a shiny "new" Corvette and a Plymouth Fury sporting graceful tail fins.

**R.E. OLDS TRANSPORTATION MUSEUM** Founded in Lansing, Oldsmobile also built millions of cars there.

This museum's extensive collection includes the first innovative Toronado, introduced in 1966, and the last Oldsmobile to come off the assembly line, a cherry-red 2004 Alero.

**WALTER P. CHRYSLER MUSEUM** Near the Chrysler headquarters in Auburn Hills, three stories of more than 65 vintage vehicles on display include 1960s muscle cars, classic Dodge pickups and a scarlet 1941 Chrysler Newport convertible.

**WOODWARD DREAM CRUISE** The third Saturday of every August, Detroit's storied Woodward Avenue (where the nation's first mile of concrete pavement was poured) hosts a 16-mile parade of primped and polished vintage cars through the city and eight suburbs.

**YPSILANTI AUTOMOTIVE HERITAGE MUSEUM** Housed in the venerable Miller Motors Hudson Dealership building, this collection includes classic Hudsons, Kaiser-Frazers, Corvairs and a replica of the innovative rear-engined 1946 Tucker.

## FIVE FABULOUS PLATES

### Flint Style@Angelo's
This Coney Island-style eatery has been a Flint landmark since 1949. Ask for a Coney dog Flint-style to get a less-juicy meat-sauce topping.

### Heritage Favorites@ Michigan Cafe
Cherry-chicken-sausage, pasties (meat pies) and pulled pork are among regional classics served in the cafeteria of The Henry Ford in Dearborn.

### Authentic Dining@ Eagle Tavern
Dine on authentic 19th-century fare like beef cakes, pork and apple pie, and squash soup served by costumed waiters in Greenfield Village's 1831 stagecoach tavern.

### Prime Rib@English Inn
Beef comes with a side of Yorkshire pudding at this posh Eaton Rapids restaurant, pub and bed and breakfast 18 miles south of Lansing.

### Burgers@Sidetrack Bar & Grill
Near the Ypsilanti Automotive Heritage Museum, Sidetrack draws a crowd for its build-your-own burgers. The tin ceiling, exposed brick and hardwood floors add charm.

Chocolate and pecans combine in this rich dessert. *(Below, from left)* Admiring Buicks at Flint's Alfred P. Sloan Museum. Vintage cars are showcased like fine gems in Auburn Hills' Walter P. Chrysler Museum.

# MILLIONAIRE'S PIE

*You can bank on it: This Greenfield Village favorite is a rich dessert. A wedge of this walnut, coconut and chocolate pie tastes like a million bucks. Just mix, layer, pour and pop in the oven.*

Prep: 35 minutes  Bake: 50 minutes  Cool: 2 hours

½ of a 15-ounce package (1 crust) rolled refrigerated unbaked piecrust
3 eggs, lightly beaten
1 cup light-color corn syrup
⅓ cup granulated sugar
⅓ cup packed brown sugar
⅓ cup butter, melted
1 teaspoon vanilla
¼ teaspoon salt
1 cup semisweet chocolate pieces
1 cup flaked coconut
1 cup coarsely chopped walnuts or pecans
Whipped cream and shaved chocolate (optional)

1. Let piecrust stand according to package directions. Unroll piecrust; place into a 9-inch pie plate. Tuck piecrust under and flute edges. Do not prick the piecrust. Set aside.
2. For filling: In a medium bowl, combine the eggs, corn syrup, granulated sugar, brown sugar, butter, vanilla and salt.
3. Layer semisweet chocolate pieces, coconut and walnuts in piecrust. Pour filling over chocolate mixture, spreading evenly. To prevent overbrowning, cover the edge of the pie with foil.
4. Bake in a 350° oven for 30 minutes. Remove foil; bake for 20 to 25 minutes more or until center appears set when you shake pie gently. Cool completely on a wire rack. Cover and store in the refrigerator within 2 hours.
5. If you like, serve with whipped cream and sprinkle with shaved chocolate. **Makes 8 to 10 servings.**

TIP: For a classic flute, place one of your thumbs against the inside edge of the pastry. Using the thumb and index finger of your other hand, press the pastry from the outside into your first thumb to form a crimp. Continue around the edge.

## Calling classic-car lovers

All of us have car stories. Few of them are better than Jack Miller's yarn. Jack, a big man with a broad grin, is the curator of the Ypsilanti Automotive Heritage Museum in the historic Depot Town. He's also part of the collection. The museum and its 30 classic cars occupy the world's last Hudson dealership. Jack was its proprietor.

"I started here in 1953, when I was 14, working for my dad," he says. "I saw it all."

Today, the former dealership draws classic-car lovers. The old showroom displays a mint 1953 two-tone green Hudson Super Jet, built just four years before the Hudson nameplate was dropped and the company merged with Nash to form American Motors. One bay in the museum holds a replica Tucker from the 1988 movie *Tucker: The Man and His Dream,* about the innovative car designed by Ypsilanti native Preston Tucker.

PHOTOGRAPHS: BOB STEFKO. (OPPOSITE, CLOCKWISE FROM TOP) ANDY LYONS; BOB STEFKO (2)

*(From left)* Family-style meals are the hallmark at Zehnder's of Frankenmuth. Travel through town in a horse-drawn carriage.

# A Taste of Bavaria in Frankenmuth

ALONG THE BANKS of the Cass River, Frankenmuth opens up a storybook world of fun and old-world charm. Settled by German immigrants in 1845, this village holds on to some of the most appealing features of its heritage, including Bavarian-themed shops, inns, restaurants, breweries and wineries.

Nutcrackers and cuckoo clocks fill store shelves and display windows. German oompah bands and strolling minstrels entertain in parks and plazas, and bright blooms cascade from 400 hanging flower baskets. Horse-drawn carriages roll along streets; paddle-wheel riverboats ply the village's waterways.

Families who return year after year to Little Bavaria (population 4,800; 93 miles northwest of Detroit) treasure memories of gathering on Sunday afternoons for all-you-can-eat chicken dinners at the German-style Bavarian Inn Restaurant or Early-American-themed Zehnder's of Frankenmuth Restaurant.

Newcomers who have never heard a glockenspiel or walked over a wooden bridge or danced the *Beer Barrel Polka* discover the traditions of a community that's never lost touch with its roots.

While one foot remains firmly in the past, Frankenmuth looks toward the future. Every year, the town rolls out new attractions. This mix of old and new, familiar and unfamiliar keeps visitors coming back and makes every trip an adventure. It's no wonder Frankenmuth attracts some 3 million visitors annually, making it Michigan's most-visited town.

## TASTES GUIDE

Day trips, weekend getaways and vacation stays begin at the centrally located Fischer Platz in the shadow of the Bavarian Inn Restaurant. Every hour, the 35-bell carillon plays German melodies while carved wooden figurines reenact the legend of the Pied Piper of Hamelin. For details, visit michigan.org.

**BAVARIAN INN RESTAURANT** For generations, families have gathered around heaping platters of fried chicken, served by waiters in lederhosen and waitresses in white aprons and caps. Schnitzel and sauerbraten add German flavor.

**CHOCOLATES & MORE** The *more* in this candy shop is a selection of Michigan-made wines from Wolcott Winery. Enjoy a wine and chocolate tasting in the store or on a Cass River cruise aboard an electric FunShip.

*(Right)* Rollicking traditional music stars at a year-long line-up of festivals.

Settled by German immigrants in 1845, this village holds on to some of the most appealing features of its heritage, including Bavarian-themed shops, inns, restaurants, breweries and wineries. Nutcrackers and cuckoo clocks fill store shelves.

**FRANKENMUTH CHEESE HAUS** Sample while you shop your way through displays of aged cheddar, Swiss and other cheeses, plus wines and jams.

**FRANKENMUTH FUDGE KITCHEN** Watch the staff pour fudge from large copper kettles onto marble tables and then shape it into loaves. Choose from 21 flavors.

**TIFFANY'S FOOD & SPIRITS** The hand-tossed pasta, pizza, seafood and brats taste even better on the shady patio of this turn-of-the-century restaurant and pub. Add a stein of German brew.

**WILLI'S SAUSAGE COMPANY** Meat cases brim with more than 100 kinds of sausage, including German ring sausage, bockwurst and brats. Add beef, turkey and buffalo jerky to your cart.

**ZEHNDER'S OF FRANKENMUTH** Stately white pillars and family-style chicken dinners are the hallmarks of this Early-American-themed restaurant that serves nearly 1 million guests annually in its 10 dining rooms. Take home breads and pastries from the bakery in the expansive marketplace.

## BETWEEN MEALS

**BAVARIAN BELLE** Board the ornate 150-passenger paddle wheeler at the waterfall at River Place for a one-hour narrated cruise on the Cass River. The *Belle* is an authentic flat-bottomed riverboat.

**FRANKENMUTH CARRIAGE COMPANY** Sit back and enjoy the sights via an old-fashioned horse-drawn carriage. Your driver will point out historic landmarks, shops and restaurants.

**MC CELLAN'S FRANKENMUTH WOOLEN MILL** See workers wash and card wool; shop the 117-year-old mill's assortment of colorful wool-filled comforters, open daily.

**ZEHNDER'S SPLASH VILLAGE HOTEL & WATERPARK** Just south of downtown, this family-oriented inn features a 30,000-square-foot indoor water park offering four-story tube slides, a dumping bucket and a lazy river.

Made-from-scratch Bavarian muffins and corn sticks. For recipe, see page 149. *(Below, from left)* Frankenmuth Clock Company stocks more than 1,000 different kinds. Standing guard outside Bavarian Inn's Castle Shops.

# BAVARIAN HONEY-BRAN MUFFINS

*Local restaurants tap Frankenmuth's restored 1848 mill for flour. The family-owned Bavarian Inn highlights local ingredients in a variety of from-scratch breads, its signature item being the Bavarian Honey-Bran Muffins.*

Prep: 15 minutes  Bake: 16 minutes

 2 cups all-purpose flour
 2 cups unprocessed wheat bran
¾ cup raisins
¼ cup sugar
1¼ teaspoons baking soda
¼ teaspoon salt
 1 egg, lightly beaten
¾ cup milk
⅔ cup honey
½ cup butter, melted

**1.** Line sixteen 2½-inch muffin cups with paper bake cups. Set aside. In a large bowl, combine flour, wheat bran, raisins, sugar, baking soda and salt. Make a well in center of flour mixture; set aside.

**2.** In a small bowl, combine egg, milk, honey and melted butter. Add egg mixture to flour mixture. Stir just until moistened (batter should be lumpy).

**3.** Spoon the batter into the prepared muffin cups, filling each two-thirds full. Bake in a 400° oven for 16 to 18 minutes or until golden brown and a wooden toothpick inserted in centers comes out clean. Cool in muffin cups on a wire rack for 5 minutes. Remove from muffin cups. Serve warm.

**Makes 16 muffins.**

**TIP:** Syrup, honey and molasses cling to the inside of a measuring cup, making it necessary to scrape out the liquid with a spatula. Skip that sticky step by first spraying the empty measuring cup with nonstick cooking spray. The syrup, honey or molasses will flow cleanly from the cup for a mess-free measure.

**TIP:** Honey that has become crystallized or cloudy can be made clear and smooth again. Place the jar of honey in a container of warm water, and occasionally stir the honey until the crystals dissolve. Change the warm water as necessary.

## Making merry all year long

Bronner's CHRISTmas Wonderland, the world's largest Christmas store, re-creates the magic of Santa's North Pole workshop. Each year, more than 2 million shoppers gaze at two 17-foot-tall Santas and equally expansive snowman before entering the massive Frankenmuth store. Once through the doors, they surrender themselves to holiday cheer that includes carolers and dancing Santas.

The 2.2-acre showroom is a glittering maze of decorated trees; ornaments of every possible shape, size and color; nativities from around the world; collectible Hummel figurines and more.

Honoring the birthplace of one of the most beloved Christmas carols, Bronner's also welcomes visitors to a replica of the original Silent Night Memorial Chapel in Oberndorf, Austria.

# BRATS AND BEER CHEDDAR CHOWDER

*As the temperature drops, comfort food beckons with promises of warmth and flavor. This filling chowder honors the town's German heritage. The tang of the beer and the smokiness of the brats balance the bold cheddar and caraway.*

Start to finish: 45 minutes

2  tablespoons butter
1  medium onion, finely chopped
1  medium carrot, coarsely shredded
3  large shallots, chopped
1  14-ounce can vegetable broth
⅓  cup all-purpose flour
1  cup half-and-half or light cream
1  teaspoon caraway seeds, crushed
¼  teaspoon ground black pepper
2½  cups shredded sharp cheddar cheese (10 ounces)
12  ounces cooked smoked bratwurst or Polish sausage, halved lengthwise and sliced
1  12-ounce can beer or one 12-ounce bottle ale
   Shredded sharp cheddar cheese (optional)

**1.** In a large saucepan, heat butter over medium heat. Add onion, carrot and shallots; reduce heat to medium-low. Cook for 10 to 15 minutes or until onion is very soft and golden, stirring frequently.
**2.** In a large screw-top jar, combine broth and flour. Cover and shake until smooth. Stir broth mixture into onion mixture. Add half-and-half, caraway seeds and pepper. Cook over medium heat about 5 minutes or until mixture is thickened, stirring frequently.
**3.** Gradually stir in the 2½ cups cheese; reduce heat to low. Cook and stir until cheese is melted. (Do not boil.) Stir in brats and beer. Cook until heated through, stirring frequently.
**4.** To serve, ladle soup into warmed soup bowls. If you like, garnish with additional shredded cheese.
**Makes 4 to 6 servings.**

TIP: Cool soup before refrigerating. Place the saucepan in a sink of ice water and stir the soup so it cools quickly. For short-term storage, divide cooled soup or stew among shallow containers. Cover and chill in the refrigerator for up to 3 days.

## Brewing up tradition

The Frankenmuth Brewery not only symbolizes the town's long tradition of German beer brewing but also occupies a prime and scenic location overlooking the meandering Cass River. The riverside tables on its tiered outdoor patios offer the best seats in town for chowing down on hearty pub grub, sampling craft specialty beers and whiling away an afternoon.

The historic brewery serves more than a half-dozen beers—pilsners, pale ales and seasonal favorites—that diners match with entrees that include meat loaf sandwiches, brats and pan-fried walleye.

Founded in 1862, the brewery has withstood fire, flood, Prohibition and a tornado while welcoming new owners several times. Despite its many ups and downs, the Frankenmuth Brewery claims to be the nation's second-oldest microbrewery.

Downtown Marshall is a gem of immaculately tended historic buildings filled with modern galleries, specialty shops and restaurants.

This is still farm country—near US-12—with a relaxed, friendly attitude.

PHOTOGRAPHS: BRAD ZIEGLER (OPPOSITE) BOB STEFKO

## Rolling Hills and Stagecoach Stops

In the mid-1800s, travelers between Chicago and Detroit on the Old Chicago Road endured five days in stagecoaches. Today, you can stretch that trip as long as you like, stopping to appreciate views, roadside fare and historic towns. From the Lake Michigan shore east to near Ann Arbor, US-12 travels through small towns so tidy and well-kept that they draw double takes from passersby. Onetime stagecoach roads and 19th-century pikes also connect larger communities, among them Battle Creek, Kalamazoo and Jackson.

US-12 winds around 50-plus lakes, fens and hills, coasting past towns Irish immigrants settled in the 19th century, giving the area its nickname of the Irish Hills. Roadside arrows

point to warrens of specialty and antiques stores—so many that the region is known as Antique Alley. Dealers have set up shop in Victorian storefronts, stagecoach stops, even a one-room school. Browse more than 70 shops along the route, a living record of one of the nation's oldest roads.

With 850 buildings in its National Historic Landmark District, Marshall (population: 7,500) feels like a gateway to the past. The town boomed in the mid-1800s when speculators bet that Marshall, rather than Lansing, would be the state capital. Stints as a railroad center and patent medicine manufacturer brought more wealth and opulent homes. Marshall boasts the state's oldest operating inn, the restored 1835 National House. Beyond history and beauty, the town offers visitors a variety of specialty and antiques shops.

## FIVE FABULOUS PLATES

### Sweet Stuff@Schuler's Restaurant & Pub
The dessert menu of this Marshall establishment includes Michigan Cherry Crisp, but consider a glass of port and the coconut snowball of vanilla-bean ice cream with hot fudge.

### Fresh & Mostly Local @Food Dance
Area farms provide ingredients for dishes such as the organic pulled pork sandwich and pumpkin risotto. Visit the market and bakery of this Kalamazoo gem.

### Funky Fast@ Stevenson's Speedy Chick
The Marshall eatery is humbly yours for take-out fried chicken, smelt and many more fast-food bites.

### Publicious@Griffin Grill & Pub
Choose among 36 beers on tap, then ponder the fish and chips, corned beef and cabbage, and the big burgers served at this downtown Battle Creek establishment. Come early for breakfast.

### Scratch Made@ Froehlich's
Grab a loaf of fresh-from-the-oven bread, a jar of Michigan peach jam and head for the tables. Sandwiches and soups are also on the menu at this deli in downtown Three Oaks.

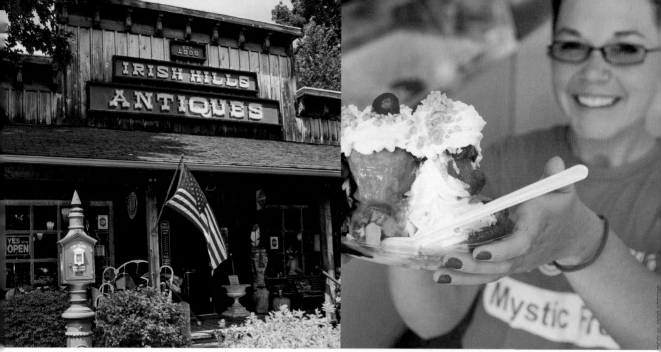

*(From left)* Visitors browse more than 70 antiques shops along US-12 in the Irish Hills. Try a banana split at Molly's in Dundee.

## TASTES GUIDE

Old and new contrast and mingle appealingly in the state's southern tier, where towns are simultaneously preserving their pasts and reinventing themselves with stunning results. Steer down two-lane roads to savor the beauty. Even larger communities set along busy interstates retain their charm and historic character.

**CHERRY CREEK VINEYARD** One of several wineries in the region, this establishment in an old one-room schoolhouse near Brooklyn also sells fruit preserves, salsas and dressings.

**DRIER'S MEAT MARKET** Since shortly after the Civil War, this Three Oaks market has satisfied generations with its bologna, smoked hams, thick-cut bacon, brats and other meats.

**MOLLY'S MYSTIC FREEZE** Sundaes and banana splits are an art form at this classic ice cream stop in Dundee.

**VIOLA CAFE** Owned and operated by two sisters, this Three Oaks eatery serves breakfast and lunch. Specials include creamed chicken and biscuits.

## BETWEEN MEALS

**AIR ZOO** Aviation buffs love this Kalamazoo museum and theme park where retired military pilots describe antique aircraft on display. Kids can fly simulators, and visitors can actually take flight in classic military craft.

**FESTIVAL OF THE FORKS** An Albion tradition since 1967, this September celebration includes a parade, classic cars, live music, art and more.

**GOVERNOR'S MANSION MUSEUM** Tour the stately 1839 mansion built in the vain hope that Marshall would became Michigan's capital.

**HONOLULU HOUSE** Visit the tropical-inspired home a former counsel to Hawaii built in 1860. It's now the headquarters of the Marshall Historical Society.

**IRISH HILLS ANTIQUES** Specializing in brass cash registers, porcelain and thousands of other items, this Brooklyn shop is one of the antiques stops along US-12 in the Irish Hills.

**MARSHALL WALKING TOUR** Stop by the chamber of commerce for a map before embarking on a self-guided tour of Marshall's National Historic Landmark District encompassing 144 buildings and 50 markers.

**WALKER TAVERN STATE HISTORIC SITE** Vintage baseball games are frequently played at the park near Brooklyn showcasing an 1840s tavern and stage stop along the old Chicago Road.

**WHITEHOUSE NATURE CENTER** Hike 7.5 miles of woodland trail past marshes and ponds in the 135-acre preserve along a branch of the Kalamazoo River in Albion.

*(From left)* Marshall's Brooks Memorial Fountain. Drier's Meat Market in Three Oaks.

US-12 winds around 50-plus lakes, fens and hills, coasting past towns Irish immigrants settled in the 19th century, giving the area its nickname of the Irish Hills. Roadside arrows point to warrens of antiques stores, so many the region is known as Antique Alley.

## HISTORIC HOSPITALITY

You're in the footsteps of generations of travelers when you step into The National House, Michigan's oldest operating inn. Established as a stagecoach stop midway along the Detroit-to-Chicago route in 1835, the Marshall inn was built with bricks fired on site and wood sawn at area mills.

Several of the 16 individually appointed guest rooms overlook the elegant Brooks Memorial Fountain, a replica of Marie Antoinette's Temple of Love at Versailles, France. The inn's central location makes it an ideal base for exploring Marshall's many antiques and specialty shops. In the lobby, guests will find The Tin Whistle Gift Shoppe. An overnight stay comes with a home-cooked full breakfast, afternoon tea and fresh popcorn in the evening.

A downtown Marshall anchor since 1909, Schuler's Restaurant is as famous for friendly service as it is for its beef entrees, baked breads and sumptuous desserts.

# CLASSIC ROAST PRIME RIB OF BEEF AU JUS

*Four generations of Schulers have nurtured Schuler's Restaurant & Pub. Fresh-baked bread and classic dishes fill the menu. This recipe combines simple ingredients with a classic side to create an old-world favorite.*

Prep: 15 minutes  Roast: 1¾ hours  Stand: 15 minutes

1  4- to 6-pound beef rib roast
   Kosher salt or salt
   Freshly ground black pepper
2  to 3 cloves garlic, slivered
   Oven-Browned Potatoes (recipe follows) (optional)
2  cups boiling water
2  teaspoons instant beef bouillon granules

**1.** Sprinkle meat with salt and pepper. Cut shallow slits all over meat and insert garlic slivers into slits. Place meat, fat side up, in a 15½x10½x2-inch roasting pan. Insert an oven-going meat thermometer into center of the meat. The thermometer should not touch bone.
**2.** Roast, uncovered, in a 350° oven. For medium rare, roast for 1¾ to 2¼ hours or until the meat thermometer registers 135°.
**3.** If you like, add Oven-Browned Potatoes to pan about 30 to 40 minutes before meat is done (the temperature of meat should be about 100°).
**4.** Remove from oven. Cover meat loosely with foil; let stand for 15 minutes before serving. Temperature of meat after standing should be 145°. (For medium, roast for 2¼ to 2¾ hours or until the meat thermometer registers 150°. Cover meat loosely with

foil; let stand for 5 minutes before serving. Temperature of meat after standing should be 160°.)
**5.** Transfer meat and Oven-Browned Potatoes to a platter. Spoon drippings from roasting pan into a small bowl; skim fat. Add the boiling water and beef bouillon granules to roasting pan, stirring and scraping crusty browned bits off the bottom. Stir in pan drippings. Cook and stir until bubbly. Season to taste. **Makes 12 to 16 servings.**

**Oven-Browned Potatoes:** Halve or quarter 3 pounds tiny new potatoes. Cook potatoes and 1 large onion, cut into thin wedges, in boiling lightly salted water for 10 minutes; drain. Toss hot potato mixture with 2 tablespoons olive oil and ½ teaspoon kosher salt or salt. Continue as directed in Step 3.

## Landmark dining

"Take the best of the past and keep it fresh," declares Hans Schuler, owner of Schuler's Restaurant & Pub in Marshall. A landmark after more than 100 years of operation, the elegant old-world restaurant holds a place in the hearts of generations.

Hans' grandfather Albert opened the restaurant in 1909, and it has occupied the Tudor-style building along Main Street since 1924.

Dining in the Centennial Room, you feel a part of the restaurant's heritage. Soft light illuminates vintage photos of Marshall on the walls. Rough-hewn wooden beams overhead bear philosophers' quotations etched in gold Gothic letters.

As soon as you're seated, a waiter delivers a basket of freshly baked breads. Swiss onion soup is a favorite starter. For the main course, the prime rib is as much of a tradition as the restaurant itself.

> 66 I love the variety of products available in the state ... and can't wait to show the rest of the country all of the things I can create using the bounty available from Michigan.
>
> — CHRIS MADSEN, AMWAY GRAND PLAZA, GRAND RAPIDS

The classic De Zwann Windmill towers 12 stories above a sea of tulips at Windmill Island Garden.

## Dutch Heritage in Holland

HOLLAND LOVES TO SHOW off its tulips, windmills and wooden shoes. And why not? This Lake Michigan community (population: 35,000; 186 miles west of Detroit) owes its favorite traditions to its old country founders.

Seeking religious tolerance and a better life, the Rev. Albertus van Raalte and 60 Calvinist immigrants established Holland in 1847 along the shores of Lake Macatawa, inland from Lake Michigan. Over time, they transformed swampy wilderness into a close-knit community embracing old-world architecture and celebrations and New World freedoms.

You'll see the Dutch touches everywhere—from the 250-year-old windmill imported from the Netherlands to the springtime eruption of color as millions of flowers bloom during the Tulip Time festival.

Holland offers much more, of course. A vibrant downtown opens off East 8th Street. Renovated historic buildings deliver an updated version of the old-fashioned Main Street, with boutiques, bookstores, coffee shops, a brewpub, restaurants and bars.

At Holland State Park, Lake Macatawa meets Lake Michigan in a preserve of sugar-sand beaches overlooked by Big Red, a much-photographed lighthouse dating to the turn of the 20th century.

### TASTES GUIDE

Navigating Holland is a breeze. The coastal town feels much smaller than it actually is because downtown's inner ring is complete with shopping, dining, coffee shops and two hotels. If you choose, the majority of a vacation can be spent on foot.

**8TH STREET GRILLE** Chicken corn chowder is always among the soup bar offerings at the casual downtown eatery that's also known for a big list of local beers and giant shakes.

**BOATWERKS WATERFRONT RESTAURANT** Great Lakes whitefish and perch are among the entrees at the renowned eatery overlooking Lake Macatawa. The house specialty is mac and cheese with aged white cheddar.

PHOTOGRAPHS: BRIAN CONFER

The Tulip Time festival brings three parades, concerts and plays, Dutch food, trolley tours and traditional Dutch dancers.

**CITYFLATS HOTEL** The downtown inn features eco-friendly decor, brunches with flatbread creations in the penthouse CityVu Bistro and espresso drinks made with fair-trade coffee at CityBrü in the lobby.

**THE CURRAGH** Take a break from all things Dutch at this downtown watering hole. Sip Guinness and Irish whiskeys while deciding whether to order the shepherd's pie or corned beef and cabbage.

**THE GOOD EARTH CAFE** This healthy breakfast and lunch haven serves from-scratch bagels, breakfast casseroles, soups and sandwiches.

**WINDMILL RESTAURANT** Hearty portions and friendly staff are a hallmark of this breakfast-all-day eatery, a downtown favorite. Fill up on from-scratch breads, omelets, hash-brown creations and cinnamon rolls.

## BETWEEN MEALS

**HOLLAND MUSEUM** Housed in a refurbished marble-floored 1914 post office building, the museum showcases local and Great Lakes historical exhibits and an extensive collection of Dutch art.

**HOLLAND STATE PARK** In addition to enjoying Lake Michigan beaches, visitors can climb the 250-plus stairs to the top of Mt. Pisgah sand dune. The Ottawa County bike trail running through the park links to 30 miles of roadside trails. The lighthouse, Big Red, can best be seen from the park.

**MACATAWA BOAT HOUSE** Rent kayaks, canoes and stand-up paddle boards at this outfitter near Holland State Park.

**NELIS' DUTCH VILLAGE** A 25-bell carillon greets visitors to this theme park and shopping complex featuring brick walkways, canals and gardens. Settle in with comfort food at the Hungry Dutchman Cafe.

**TULIP TIME FESTIVAL** This celebration includes parades, variety shows, more than 1,000 dancers, loads of Dutch food and plenty of tulips.

**VELDHEER TULIP GARDENS** The nation's largest bulb-production farm welcomes spring guests to 5 million blooming tulips. The gardens also house a delftware Dutch pottery studio and a wooden-shoe factory.

A traditional Dutch holiday favorite. *(Below, from left)* Millions of tulips bloom during Tulip Time. Holland is a modern village with busy shops, pubs and restaurants.

# DUTCH DELITE BLANKETS

*Dutch Delite Bakery's owner Ralph van Asperen of Holland bakes these traditional Netherland treats using a recipe handed down from his father.*

Prep: 1 hour  Bake: 30 minutes  Chill: 8 hours plus 15 minutes

- 1 egg, lightly beaten
- ½ of an 8-ounce can almond paste (about ½ cup)
- ½ cup sugar
- 2 tablespoons all-purpose flour
- ½ cup slivered almonds, toasted and chopped
  Butterdough (see recipe, page 150)
  Powered Sugar Icing (see recipe, page 151)

**1.** Reserve 1 tablespoon of the beaten egg; set aside. In a small mixing bowl, beat the remaining egg, almond paste, sugar and flour with an electric mixer on low to medium speed until combined. Using a wooden spoon, stir in chopped almonds. Divide mixture in half. Shape each half into a 13-inch-long almond-paste roll; set aside.
**2.** Roll the chilled Butterdough into a 14x14-inch square. Cut in half, forming two 14x7-inch rectangles.
**3.** For each pastry, place one of the almond-paste rolls onto one of the dough rectangles close to one of the long sides, leaving about ½ inch of dough at top and bottom of almond roll. Roll up each rectangle, starting from the almond-paste long side. Pinch dough to seal seams.
**4.** Transfer each pastry to an ungreased baking sheet. Shape into a circle,

joining ends; seal. Brush pastry with the reserved beaten egg.
**5.** Bake in a 375° oven for 30 to 35 minutes or until golden brown. Transfer to wire racks; cool. Drizzle with Powdered Sugar Icing. **Makes 2 pastry circles (16 to 20 servings).**

*Continued on page 150*

*Continued on page 150*

**TIP:** To toast whole nuts or large pieces, spread them in a shallow pan. Bake in a 350° oven for 5 to 10 minutes, shaking the pan once or twice. Toast finely chopped or ground nuts or sesame seeds in a dry skillet over medium heat. Stir often.

**TIP:** Almond paste is made from sweet almonds that have been finely ground and combined with sugar. It can be purchased ready-to-use for fillings in coffee cakes and pastries.

## A Dutch treat

There's no missing Windmill Island Gardens, a 36-acre oasis on the northeast edge of downtown Holland. Just keep an eye out for the 12-story-tall authentic Dutch windmill towering over the landscape.

Once there, traipse up De Zwaan ("The Swan") to take in views of the manicured gardens, dikes and canals of this popular stop that also features an antique Dutch carousel and picnic areas.

The windmill's vast blades slowly turn to provide power to stones that still grind flour, just as they did when the structure was built in the Netherlands in 1761. De Zwaan is particularly impressive in spring when it soars above a rainbow-hued sea of tens of thousands of tulips. In summer, girls in folk costumes and wooden shoes perform the *klompen* dance, a traditional folk dance.

Stop by the souvenir shop to take home a pair of wooden shoes or a pound of fudge made with real Dutch cocoa.

Horsepower is measured in actual horses on Mackinac Island, where motorized vehicles are banned.

# Classic Northern Experiences

IN THE MIDDLE of continually evolving food scenes in some of the state's most popular northern vacation spots, classics endure. In fact, all the committed food artisans seem to be learning and drawing from each other. Chefs are putting fresh, artful spins on classics, and long-time eateries are getting more creative and renewing their commitments to local ingredients and traditions.

That's happening around Traverse City and in Harbor Springs, Petoskey and Charlevoix. All three edge Little Traverse Bay, inviting visitors to sip regional wines on the porches of classic hotels and B&Bs, and then head downtown for cherry pie. In Charlevoix, you can catch a ferry for the 32-mile cruise to Beaver Island, one of Michigan's mellowest getaways.

Resting where the cobalt blue waters of Lakes Michigan and Huron mingle and squeeze between the Upper and Lower Peninsulas at the Straits of Mackinac, Mackinac Island has perhaps the most unique and charming hold on the past. The storied, white-columned Grand Hotel, a legacy from when steamships brought vacationers to the island, now looks down on the harbor where ferries full of visitors dock and on brick streets lined with century-old lilacs. Cars never have been allowed, so horse-drawn carriages, bikes and walkers provide a charismatic sort of bustle. Galleries, inns and boutiques mingle with shops selling the fudge that has become the island's signature.

Ferries arrive from gateways that have grown into destinations in their own right. Mackinaw City pulses at the Lower Peninsula's tip with carnival energy and the color of an always-busy collection of attractions, gift and souvenir shops, and eateries serving whitefish.

Across the famed 5-mile-long Mackinac Bridge, St. Ignace welcomes with the Upper Peninsula's kicked-back vibe. It's a great place to polish off a pasty, a filling meat pie that's become an Up-North tradition.

The sun sets under Mackinac Bridge, linking Michigan's Upper and Lower Peninsulas.

PHOTOGRAPHY: BRIAN CONFER

## TASTES GUIDE

For links and more ideas and details, visit michigan.org.

**AUDIE'S** In Mackinaw City, take your pick between The Family Room, a three-meals-a-day eatery showcasing pictures of the construction of the Mackinac Bridge, and the more upscale Chippewa Room.

**BESSIE'S ORIGINAL HOMEMADE PASTIES** The little red eatery in St. Ignace has been serving the hearty half-moon meat pies since 1958.

**BLUEBIRD CAFE** This legendary Leland eatery is known for sauteed or fried whitefish. Fish here is fresh from the nets of nearby Carlson's Fishery.

**DON'S DRIVE-IN** East of downtown Traverse City, the venerable eatery is famous for cherry malts and lean-forward-or-stain-your-lap burgers.

**GRAND HOTEL** Since 1887, this majestic retreat on Mackinac Island has welcomed guests with luxury accommodations, fine food and sweeping views from the world's longest front porch. Rates include elegant meals in the cruise-ship-size dining room. If you're not a guest, the best way to experience the hotel is the astoundingly opulent lunch buffet.

**KILWINS** Bonbons, brittles, truffles and other sweets tempt in this chaletlike store in Petoskey (branches in Harbor Springs and Traverse City).

**ODAWA CASINO RESORT** Gourmet fare and a 16-foot-tall wine tower detail the Petoskey casino's Sage Restaurant.

## FIVE FABULOUS PLATES

### Just Caught@Stoney Acre Grill
Varnished pine planks and logs line the dining room of this old barn, considered one of the best restaurants on Beaver Island. Order the fish, which came from Lake Michigan earlier that day.

### Dinner@The Grey Gables Inn
From seafood fondue to liver and onions to almond crème brûlée, the 75-year-old Charlevoix restaurant on Belvedere Avenue is deft at satisfying all tastes.

### Fast Fish@Scalawags
The expertly executed fish and chips star Great Lakes whitefish, as does the chowder. Perch and walleye sandwiches are also on the menu at this casual eatery in downtown Mackinaw City.

### Cookie Love@Tom's Mom's Cookies
The little pink bakery in downtown Harbor Springs serves up trays of big, oven-warm cookies, including the signature chocolate chunk.

### Coffee@Roast & Toast
Elaborately decorated out front with inlaid ceramic coffee mugs, the downtown Petoskey coffee shop also serves breakfast wraps, soups and salads.

*(From left)* Sleder's has welcomed diners since 1882. Scalawag's serves up delicious Great Lakes whitefish several ways.

**SLEDER'S TAVERN** This family-friendly Traverse City restaurant, with a moose head on the wall, opened in 1882. It's been a favorite ever since. The hamburger is ground each morning, the fries are hand cut and, if you're in the mood, tackle a basket of smelts.

**STAFFORD'S** The local hotel and dining empire operates Petoskey's elegant Perry Hotel and Bay View Inn, both with fine dining. Stafford's also offers waterfront dining at The Pier in Harbor Springs and The Weathervane, an old gristmill in Charlevoix.

**SYMONS GENERAL STORE** A huge wine cellar and one of the best cheese counters in Michigan draw visitors to this Petoskey shop.

**TERRACE INN** This 1911 inn within Petoskey's historic Bay View Village features 37 individually appointed rooms. Planked whitefish and chicken Hemingway top the dining menu.

## BETWEEN MEALS

**BOYNE RESORTS** Ski, golf or swim in the massive indoor water park at the Bavarian-style Boyne Mountain Resort in Boyne Falls. This family-run institution also operates resorts in Harbor Springs and Bay Harbor.

**CHERRY BOWL DRIVE-IN THEATRE** Come early for the broasted-chicken picnic dinner, stay late for movies under the stars at this classic 1953 establishment in Honor (25 miles southwest of Traverse City).

**KEWEENAW STAR** Board an excursion boat at the Charlevoix marina for a sunset, lighthouse or dinner cruise.

**MACKINAC ISLAND STATE PARK** Bike or hike through this forested park encompassing more than 80 percent of Mackinac Island.

**MACKINAC STATE HISTORIC PARKS** Get a combination ticket to top-notch living history experiences:

in Mackinaw City, Colonial Michilimackinac, a 1770s fort and fur-trading town; the 1892 Old Mackinac Point Lighthouse; and Historic Mill Creek Discovery Park. On the island, Fort Mackinac and several town buildings dating to the 1880s.

**MACKINAW CROSSINGS** Shops and restaurants in the Mackinaw City complex open onto a square.

**MACKINAW KITES & TOYS** Expert staff at the downtown Mackinaw City store can teach you how to master stiff shoreline breezes with your new kite.

**MUSEUM OF OJIBWA CULTURE** The St. Ignace museum features exhibits about Ojibwa traditions and hosts summer powwows and workshops.

**PETOSKEY STATE PARK** Along Little Traverse Bay, the preserve features two modern campgrounds near beaches and hunting grounds for Petoskey stones (ancient fossilized coral).

*(From left)* The 1896 Round Island Lighthouse near Mackinac Island. Bay View's Terrace Inn dining room.

All the committed food artisans seem to be learning and drawing from each other. Chefs are putting fresh, artful spins on classics, and long-time eateries are getting more creative and renewing their commitments to local ingredients and traditions.

## COMFORT AND CUISINE

A cool breeze off the blue chop of Little Traverse Bay caresses as you lounge in one of the white wicker chairs on the shady front porch of Stafford's Bay View Inn. You might be tempted to stay here forever, or at least until sunset, if it weren't for those intoxicating aromas wafting from the kitchen behind the Roselawn Dining Room.

Grandly built as a boarding house in 1886, the much-celebrated hotel, boasting a tall cupola, anchors the Bay View Historic District. The inn is known for comfort and cuisine. Mornings, the dining room is a haven of satisfying favorites, including sticky buns that live up to their name. Evenings, regional wines accompany Great Lakes fish. The Sunday brunch has been voted Michigan's best many times.

Mackinac Island's Grand Hotel serves up Victorian-Era hospitality and charm and a revered noon buffet. *(Opposite)* The fortresslike 1892 Old Mackinac Point Lighthouse helped guide generations of Great Lakes sailors through the treacherous straits.

# CHERRY-BERRY PIE

*This pie made Jesperson's a legend. Bobbe Kroll, owner, shares the cherry-berry story: She was baking a cherry pie at home for her kids, ran out of cherries and threw in some raspberries to finish it off. At that moment, pie history was made.*

Prep: 20 minutes  Bake: 1 hour  Stand: 15 minutes  Cool: 2 hours

- 3 cups frozen unsweetened pitted tart red cherries
- 1 cup frozen red raspberries
- Cherry juice or cranberry juice
- 1 15-ounce package (2 crusts) rolled refrigerated unbaked piecrust
- 2 teaspoons butter, melted
- 1¼ cups sugar
- 3 tablespoons cornstarch
- 1 tablespoon quick-cooking tapioca
- ¼ teaspoon salt
- ¼ teaspoon ground nutmeg
- 2 tablespoons butter, cut up
- 1 tablespoon lemon juice
- Milk (optional)
- Sugar (optional)
- Vanilla ice cream (optional)

**1.** Thaw frozen cherries and raspberries in a colander over a medium bowl, reserving juice. Add enough cherry juice to measure 1¼ cups.
**2.** Let piecrusts stand according to package directions. Unroll piecrusts; place one into a 9-inch pie plate. Do not prick piecrust. Brush bottom and sides with the 2 teaspoons melted butter; set aside.
**3.** For filling: In a medium saucepan, combine sugar, cornstarch, tapioca, salt and nutmeg. Add the 1¼ cups reserved juice. Cook and stir until thickened and bubbly. Remove from heat. Stir in the 2 tablespoons butter, the lemon juice and thawed cherries and raspberries.
**4.** Pour the filling into the piecrust-lined pie plate. Trim bottom piecrust to edge of pie plate. Cut slits in remaining piecrust; place on filling. Tuck the top piecrust under the bottom piecrust edge and seal. Flute as desired.
*Continued on page 149*

## Save room for dessert!

Don't leave Petoskey without digging into a slice of pie at Jesperson's Restaurant. Life's too short to live with the regrets. At this beloved downtown eatery on Howard Street, your only dilemma will be whether to end lunch with a wedge of the plush coconut cream or the sticky-sweet cherry-berry (they're raspberries) crowned with vanilla ice cream.

Jesperson's has been part of the Petoskey community since 1903, back when Ernest Hemingway was a loyal diner. His family kept a summer place on nearby Walloon Lake.

Bobbe Kroll, current owner and granddaughter of the founding family, seems to know everyone who enters the restaurant. She greets, while her business partner, Bill Fraser, bakes—up to 150 pies daily at the peak of the summer season.

Downtown Mackinac Island bustles. *(Above, from left)* No visit is complete without a stop to watch fudge making at a classic shop like Joann's Fudge. Decadent slices of fudge.

# EASY COCOA FUDGE

*The sweet smell of fudge drifts in the air on Mackinac Island. If you can't get there to snack on some of the original, make it yourself. Once you've mastered the basics, move on to Easy Cherry-Cocoa or Easy Latte-Cocoa fudge.*

Prep: 25 minutes  Chill: 2 hours

  1  16-ounce package (4 cups) powdered sugar
  ½  cup unsweetened European-style (Dutch processed) cocoa powder or unsweetened cocoa powder
  ½  cup butter
  ¼  cup water
  ½  cup buttermilk powder or nonfat dry milk powder
  1  teaspoon vanilla
  ½  cup chopped walnuts or pecans (optional)

**1.** Line an 8x8x2-inch baking pan with foil, extending foil over edges of pan. Butter foil; set pan aside.
**2.** In a large bowl, sift together powdered sugar and cocoa powder. (If mixture seems lumpy, sift again.)
**3.** In a small saucepan, combine the ½ cup butter and the water. Cook over medium heat until butter is just melted. Whisk in buttermilk powder. Continue cooking over medium heat just to boiling, whisking mixture until smooth. Remove pan from heat. Whisk in vanilla. Stir melted butter mixture into the powdered sugar mixture. Add chopped nuts, if you like, stirring until well combined.
**4.** Immediately transfer fudge mixture to the prepared pan. Using your hands, press mixture evenly into pan. While fudge is warm, score it into 1-inch squares. Cover and chill for 2 to 3 hours or until firm.
**5.** When fudge is firm, use foil to lift it out of pan. Cut fudge into squares. Store tightly covered in the refrigerator for up to 1 month. **Makes 64 pieces.**

**Easy Cherry-Cocoa Fudge:** Prepare as above, except in Step 3, substitute ¼ cup chopped pecans and ¼ cup snipped dried tart red cherries or dried cranberries for the ½ cup chopped walnuts.

**Easy Latte-Cocoa Fudge:** Prepare as above, except in Step 3, add 1 tablespoon instant espresso coffee powder or instant coffee crystals, an additional 1 tablespoon water and ¼ teaspoon ground cinnamon with the buttermilk powder.

## Take home a sweet souvenir

At least three Mackinac Island shops claim to be the oldest making fudge, the area's signature treat. All have their followings. The fun is in tasting and watching cooks work with slabs of creamy confection, often on marble-top tables.

As soon as you clamber off a ferryboat at the docks of the island town, you'll see fudge signs almost everywhere. Murdick's, Joann's and Ryba's are just three of the nearly two-dozen popular shops.

Flavors range from orange truffle to coffee liqueur, but the stalwarts remain vanilla, maple, chocolate and peanut butter. Buy some, and join the ranks of "fudgies," the tongue-in-cheek nickname for island visitors. Every August, thousands of people gather for Mackinac's fudge festival.

After you've had your fill of fudge, rent a bicycle or put on some good walking shoes to explore the rest of the island.

> "Little things like tasting freshly made cider, or seeing asparagus and morels pop into season, remind me of why I cook. The ability to acquire fresh Michigan produce during the different seasons really made me appreciate the seasonality of food."

— KEVIN HEE, BOURBON STEAK AND SALTWATER, DETROIT

Michigan's Lake Huron coastline earns its nickname as the Sunrise Side.

Broad beaches are summer shrines near Tawas Point.

# Northeast's Relaxed Attitude

KISSED BY TURQUOISE WATERS, the snow-white beaches of Lake Huron are seldom out of sight as you explore the Lower Peninsula's eastern shore. From Cheboygan south to Bay City, US-23 eases through communities that began life as lumber towns and fishing settlements.

Now, with kids lined up at ice cream stands, kites flying and beach toys scattered around old-time cottage resorts, the towns resemble scenes from 1960s family vacation movies. Their shaded streets end at the big lake, where all sorts of pleasure craft and fishing boats bob in marinas.

Moving inland, along the Au Sable River, northeast Michigan's character shifts from lakeshore to forests and streams, ski and golf resorts.

Along the northern shore, Alpena welcomes divers to explore more than 100 shipwrecks off the shore in the Thunder Bay National Marine Sanctuary. The wrecks, along with nearly a dozen lighthouses, are a legacy of the sometimes-violent moods of *La Mer Douce*—the sweet sea—as early French explorers dubbed Lake Huron.

Summers are lively in Tawas City and East Tawas, where cottages extend north from Tawas Point State Park, the region's most popular destination.

Bay City's downtown shops, restaurants and several parks line the Saginaw River, which links this city of 38,000 to Saginaw Bay.

Inland, baskets of pink petunias dangle from old-fashioned lampposts along Main Street in Gaylord, which, with a population of 4,000, is the region's largest interior community.

## FIVE FABULOUS PLATES

### Beef 'n' Brews@John A. Lau Saloon
Slice into steaks nightly and prime rib on weekends. Several Michigan microbrews top the big beer list at this historic Alpena saloon.

### Gourmet Glide@ Garland Lodge & Resort
Fuel up on chef-made fare like chowder, pan-fried trout and plenty of sweets at five buffet stations along the resort's 7-kilometer cross-country ski trail near Lewiston.

### Opulent Omelets@ Mornin' at Maggie's
This downtown Bay City eatery draws diners with innovative omelets and frittatas, including red pepper, Asiago and sausage, pear and gorgonzola.

### Tasty Tradition@Sugar Bowl Restaurant
A Main Street fixture since 1919, this Gaylord restaurant serves up lumberjack-size breakfasts of corned beef hash and pancakes. Other classics include Great Lakes fish and Greek dishes like *saganaki* and lemon rice.

### Double Single@ Marion's Dairy Bar
Ask for a single dip at this always-busy East Tawas ice cream shop, and you get two scoops. Makes sense to your sweet tooth. Tip: The waffle cones are from scratch.

*(From left)* A single means two scoops at Marion's Dairy Bar in East Tawas. You can climb the 1870 New Presque Isle Lighthouse.

## TASTES GUIDE

The Sunrise Side is sometimes referred to as the quiet side of Michigan due to its laid-back vibe, not-too-crowded beaches and affordable lodgings.

There's plenty of room for travelers to set their own pace and do their own thing, whether that's exploring a park, climbing the stairs of a lighthouse or stopping by a restaurant for a Friday night fish fry.

**BIG BEAR DELICATESSEN** Sandwiches and from-scratch pastries and pie come with a view of a carved bear out front and bear accents inside this Gaylord house-turned-eatery.

**THE CELLAR** Along Alpena's riverfront, this special-occasion gem serves spot-on meats and pastas. The Korean ribs are fall-off-the-bone perfect, served with garlicky fries and cabbage. On weekends, live music fills the room, which overlooks Thunder Bay River.

**DAWSON & STEVENS CLASSIC '50S DINER** You know you've stumbled onto something when you hear the diner's doo-wop soundtrack outside. Welcome to Grayling's retro diner with original pharmacy soda fountain. All the menu items are named for songs.

**FRESH PALATE** A few tables in a small atrium make up this downtown Alpena restaurant with an upstairs gallery. The menu boasts a huge selection of healthy, flavorful sandwiches, wraps and salads.

**GREAT LAKES GRILL** This popular Cheboygan family restaurant hosts fish fries on Fridays and serves fried chicken on Sundays.

**OLD CITY HALL** Bay City's former city hall takes on a second life with a lively bar scene and restaurant. Local art adorns the brick walls. The signature tomato bisque has the requisite kick as does the Bloody Mary.

**PLATH'S MEATS** For 98 years, this family-owned Rogers City shop has supplied meats and a huge variety of sausage to northeast Michigan. Make sure to try the tender smoked pork loin, by the pound or in sandwiches.

**VILLAGE CHOCOLATIER** Handmade truffles, creams, a dozen flavors of from-scratch fudge and chocolate-caramel apples make this downtown East Tawas shop a sumptuous stop.

## BETWEEN MEALS

**APPLEDORE IV** Sightseeing and dinner cruises on the Bay City-based schooner sail up the Saginaw River into Saginaw Bay.

**GARLAND LODGE & RESORT** Inland, near Lewiston, the resort boasts four golf courses, cross-country skiing, snowmobiling, a giant log lodge and midwinter horse-drawn sleigh rides followed by five-course dinners.

*(From left)* Shopping at Enchanted Blooms in Oscoda. Permanently moored in Cheboygan, the *Mackinaw* welcomes visitors.

The Sunrise Side has a laid-back vibe, not-too-crowded beaches and affordable lodgings. There's plenty of room for travelers to set their own pace and do their own thing, whether that's exploring a park or climbing the stairs of a lighthouse.

**HARTWICK PINES STATE PARK** South of Grayling, trails wind under the canopy of a 50-acre virgin forest of white pines, some 150 feet tall. Tour a replica 19th-century lumber camp.

**LUMBERMAN'S MONUMENT** Honoring lumberjacks who harvested Michigan's wealth of timber, the statue and park overlook the Au Sable River about 10 miles inland from Oscoda.

**NEW PRESQUE ISLE LIGHTHOUSE** North of Alpena, you can huff up the spiraling, 130-step staircase to the top of this 109-foot-tall 1870 tower for a view of Lake Huron and the countryside.

**P.H. HOEFT STATE PARK** Groves of white pines and hardwoods shading a campground open onto a lightly used Lake Huron beach. A paved 4.5-mile recreational trail traces the Lake Huron shore south to the restaurants and shops of Rogers City.

**STURGEON POINT LIGHTHOUSE** Near Harrisville, visit the museum in the lightkeeper's house and climb a staircase to the top of the operational 70-foot-tall tower built in 1870.

**TAWAS POINT STATE PARK** Opening across a spit of sand just north of East Tawas, the 183-acre preserve includes an 1876 lighthouse rising above a 2-mile arc of Lake Huron beach, campgrounds and woodland trails.

**THUNDER BAY RESORT** A stay at this inland resort near Hillman can include 18 holes of golf. Sit back and spot elk during a horse-drawn carriage ride to a woodland cabin for a gourmet meal cooked on wood stoves.

**TREETOPS RESORT** Near Gaylord, play five championship-caliber golf courses during the summer and downhill ski on 23 runs in winter.

**U.S. COAST GUARD CUTTER MACKINAW** Tour this 290-foot Great Lakes icebreaker permanently moored in Cheboygan after a 62-year career cracking channels into lake ice with 10,000-horsepower engines.

# LEMON AND DILL WALLEYE SANDWICHES

*Baking and frying have their merits, but grilled walleye is tasty and healthy. This easy sandwich is great for tailgating or summer parties. A lemony dill-pickle tartar sauce tops this fish sandwich.*
Prep: 1 hour  Grill: 10 minutes

1½  to 2¼ ounces fresh or frozen skinless, boneless walleye pike, haddock, sole, tilapia or cod fillets, ¾ inch thick
2   teaspoons finely shredded lemon peel
3   tablespoons lemon juice
3   tablespoons olive oil
2   tablespoons snipped fresh dill or 1 teaspoon dried dillweed
4   cloves garlic, minced
¼   teaspoon bottled hot pepper sauce
4   large lemons, cut into ¼-inch-thick slices
12  slices wheat country bread, lightly buttered
3   cups packaged shredded cabbage with carrot (coleslaw mix)
6   tomato slices
    Tartar Sauce (see recipe, page 149)

**1.** Thaw fish, if frozen. Rinse fish; pat dry. Sprinkle both sides of fish with salt and pepper.
**2.** In a small bowl, combine lemon peel, lemon juice, oil, dill, garlic and hot pepper sauce. Set aside.
**3.** For a charcoal grill: Arrange a bed of lemon slices on greased grill rack directly over medium coals. Arrange fish on lemon slices. Brush fish with the oil mixture. Cover and grill for 10 to 12 minutes or until fish flakes easily when tested with a fork. Do not turn fish. (For a gas grill: Preheat grill. Reduce heat to medium. Arrange lemon slices and fish on greased grill rack

over heat. Brush fish with oil mixture. Cover and grill as above.) Place bread, cut side down, next to fish for last 2 minutes of grilling, turning bread slices once.
**4.** To serve, top six of the bread slices or bun bottoms with shredded cabbage and tomato slices. Top with the fish pieces and Tartar Sauce. Cover with the six bread tops. Discard the lemon slices. **Makes 6 sandwiches.**
*Continued on page 149*

*Continued on page 149*

## Chocolates with a twist

Salty and sweet can be a very good thing, particularly when the sweet involves chocolate. That's why ripple potato chips tucked in a thick coating of milk chocolate are the best-selling snacks at the Alpine Chocolat Haus in downtown Gaylord.

Owner Bruce Brown is equally proud of his Alpine Crunch—a layer of caramel corn and a layer of chips topped with a rich dose of a two-tone chocolate drizzle.

All the chocolate treats are handmade upstairs in Bruce's little candy factory. Other favorites include chocolate-covered cherries, marshmallow cups and hefty 4-ounce bear paws made with milk chocolate, cashews and caramel. If you're a fan of crispy rice cereal bars, make sure to try Bruce's on-a-stick versions. They're covered in chocolate, of course.

Woods, water and solitude are key ingredients of a getaway on the vast, lightly populated Upper Peninsula. Here a hiker views

## The Upper Peninsula's Rugged Beauty

FORESTS, WATERFALLS, BEACHES, mountains, sand dunes and cliffs endure mostly untouched on this rugged 350-mile-long wedge of land flanked by three Great Lakes.

The largest city, Marquette, an energetic onetime mining capital making a comeback with lakefront parks and condos, has a population of only 19,600. Next come a handful of towns like Sault Ste. Marie, where building-size freighters nudge through the Soo Locks in the busy international harbor, and Houghton and Hancock, split by a shipping

channel that dates to mining boom days. Other communities barely make dents in a wilderness rich with inspiring sights.

The mineral-stained cliffs and sand dunes of Pictured Rocks National Lakeshore stretch for 42 miles along the Lake Superior shore. Trails lead to waterfalls, empty beaches and rock formations. Tahquamenon Falls, five stories high and 200 feet wide, roars to the south. On the UP's west side, Porcupine Mountains Wilderness State Park encompasses peaks, waterfalls, secluded glacial lakes, miles of rivers and streams, and old-growth forest. Hikers seek out 90 miles of trails with just the right mix of challenge and striking scenery.

### TASTES GUIDE

Much of the Upper Peninsula feels almost unchanged since early Native Americans hunted vast forests and traveled pristine rivers. You can follow in their footsteps to adventure—dip a paddle, explore a trail or simply savor this region's unspoiled character. Don't rule out a winter visit. With an annual average of 200 inches of snow covering trails and slopes, there are few better places to revel in the white stuff. UP'ers also know how to warm you up—from welcoming inns and cafes to toasty saunas, all at prices reasonable enough to feed the glow. **BIG BAY POINT LIGHTHOUSE BED AND BREAKFAST** The 1896 light tower with guest rooms in the adjoining

Lake of the Clouds in the Porcupine Mountains.

## FIVE FABULOUS PLATES

### The Big C@Clyde's Drive-In
Chow down on this monster ¾-pound burger at a picnic table while you watch Great Lakes freighters chug past this classic 1949 burger joint in Sault Ste. Marie.

### FineFare@Capers
Start with the baked Brie with Michigan cherries then move on to the grilled Great Lakes trout at this comfortably elegant restaurant in Marquette's waterfront Landmark Inn Hotel.

### Local Flavor@The Buck Inn
The Bay De Noc Platter features local walleye, whitefish and perch served in an Escanaba restaurant and tavern that's been a UP favorite since 1935.

### Muffin Love@Babycakes Muffin Company
Go healthy with the bran date nut muffin—or not with the sour cream chocolate chip. Scones, quiche, bread and rolls also are made from-scratch daily in this downtown Marquette bakery and cafe.

### The Original@Joe's Pasty Shop
Since 1946, this humble downtown Ironwood eatery has served countless thousands of hearty meat pies. Try the breakfast and veggie pasties.

lightkeeper's home commands a cliff jutting into Lake Superior near Big Bay. Guests can climb to the lighthouse lantern 120 feet above.

CASA CALABRIA Laid-back yet elegant dining is what you'll find at Marquette's Italian and steak restaurant. Choose from perfectly grilled steaks and fresh-made pasta, or there's an extensive pizza and sandwich menu for every taste.

HILLTOP FAMILY RESTAURANT The famous cinnamon rolls at the L'Anse cafe tip the scales at over a pound. If you're in a savory mood, try the gravy-smothered meat loaf.

MT. SHASTA Fresh Lake Superior trout and whitefish star at this North Woods diner in Michigamme.

PASTY POWER Indulge at these meat-pie shrines: Bessie's in St. Ignace, Dobber's in Escanaba, Jean Kay's in Marquette, Joe's in Ironwood, Muldoon's in Munising, Randall's in Wakefield and Toni's in Laurium.

SUOMI RESTAURANT AND BAKERY This Houghton eatery is a favorite breakfast stop for locals. The fare includes Finnish accents such as French toast made with Finnish egg bread and *pannukakku*, a puffy, custardlike pancake.

TERRACE BAY RESORT Catering to Little Bay de Noc anglers, the Lake Michigan inn between Gladstone and Escanaba enjoys a colorful history as a 1930s dance hall. The Surf Room restaurant features an outdoor bar.

Taking in the action at the Soo Locks in Sault Ste. Marie from the viewing platform of the 210-foot-tall Tower of History.

## BETWEEN MEALS

**DA YOOPERS TOURIST TRAP & MUSEUM** Take a turn at the giant chain saw west of Ishpeming to join the fun—a zany deer camp display, a pickup-truck-mounted working rifle the size of a howitzer and loads of gag gifts at this souvenir store.

**DOWNHILL SKIING** Choose among nearly a dozen resorts, most offering ski schools, terrain parks, lodging and après ski activities. Among them: Big Powderhorn and Blackjack near Bessemer, Indianhead near Wakefield, Pine Mountain Resort at Iron Mountain, Porcupine at Ontonagon, and Ski Brule at Iron River.

**GREAT LAKES SHIPWRECK MUSEUM AT WHITEFISH POINT** In Paradise, the complex features a restored light tower, crew quarters, and exhibits about the *Edmund Fitzgerald* and almost 200 others that didn't make it around the treacherous point.

**HOUGHTON WINTER CARNIVAL** Ice sculptures highlight this February celebration that also features curling, cross-country ski and snowshoe races, and a torchlight parade.

**INTERNATIONAL 500 SNOWMOBILE RACE** The best sled drivers in the world compete at this February race on a 1.5-mile oval track.

**ISLE ROYALE NATIONAL PARK** Take ferries or planes from Houghton and Copper Harbor to this remote Lake Superior island to canoe, kayak, hike, and soak up peace and quiet.

**LAKE SUPERIOR THEATRE** Four summer plays are staged in the Frazier Historic Boat House along the scenic shore of Marquette.

**LAURIUM MANOR INN** In Laurium on the Keweenaw Peninsula, quirky charms appoint this hotel in a 1908 mansion. The thermostat on a rare original heating system lists 98 degrees as "blood heat."

**LES CHENEAUX ISLANDS ANTIQUE WOODEN BOAT SHOW** Always in mid-August in Hessel, the show features dozens of classic wood vessels, ranging from mahogany racing boats to steam-powered launches. The Les Cheneaux Maritime Museum also shows off several classic vessels.

Wind and water sculpted the sandstone of Pictured Rocks National Lakeshore.

**MARQUETTE MARITIME MUSEUM** At this waterfront museum, discover Great Lakes history and the best collection of lighthouse lenses. Tour the adjacent 1866 lighthouse and get a glimpse of what a keeper's life was like.

**MOUNT BOHEMIA** Rip down tree-studded triple-black-diamond plunges at this extreme skiing hot spot on the Keweenaw Peninsula. The resort boasts 900 feet of vertical drop, 275 inches of annual snow and no beginners' runs.

**PICTURED ROCKS NATIONAL LAKESHORE** Trails and overlooks showcase mineral-stained sandstone cliffs and rock formations extending from Munising to Grand Marais. Get up close in kayaks or excursion boats.

**QUINCY MINE HOIST NATIONAL HISTORIC PARK** Travel 400 feet under the Keweenaw Peninsula in Hancock for a copper mine tour. Take a tram ride to one of the world's finest mineral collections at the Seaman Mineralogical Museum.

**SOO LOCKS BOAT TOURS** Take a two-hour cruise exploring and making a passage through the largest waterway traffic system on Earth, where 1,000-foot-long Great Lakes freighters pass to and from Lake Superior in Sault Ste. Marie, Michigan's oldest city.

**TAHQUAMENON FALLS STATE PARK** This 45,000-acre preserve near Paradise features the dramatic Upper and Lower falls, a 40-mile network of hiking and cross-country skiing trails, four campgrounds, canoeing and horseback riding. At the park entrance, Tahquamenon Falls Brewery & Pub dishes up pasta, soups and pasties, or choose from entrees like steak, pork and shrimp scampi.

**TOWER OF HISTORY** Rising 210 feet above the Soo Locks in Sault Ste. Marie, the tower's observation deck provides high views of the lock. The lower level houses a museum of local and Native American history.

**UP 200 & MIDNIGHT RUN SLED DOG RACES** Stake out a prime viewing spot in downtown Marquette for the night start of the mid-February race that pits 12-dog teams and expert drivers on a 200-plus-mile course. Afterward, settle in for a weekend of festivities.

Much of the Upper Peninsula feels almost unchanged since early Native Americans hunted vast forests and traveled pristine rivers. You can follow in their footsteps to adventure— dip a paddle, explore a trail or simply savor this region's unspoiled character.

PHOTOGRAPH: JASON LINDSEY

The multihued hollows and clefts of Pictured Rocks National Lakeshore draw sea kayakers and excursion boat sightseers.

Peat adds a caramel hue to water flowing over the Upper and Lower Tahquamenon Falls. *(Above)* Pasties are the UP's comfort food.

# QUICK AND EASY PASTIES

*A staple in Munising, these often mispronounced pies are made by the hundreds every day. What's not so clear is the perfect topping. Ketchup, gravy, pickles? Decide for yourself. This shortcut version is perfect when time is scarce and leftovers plentiful.*

Prep: 25 minutes  Bake: 20 minutes

½  of a 15-ounce package (1 crust) rolled refrigerated unbaked piecrust
⅔  cup chopped cooked beef, pork, veal and/or lamb
⅔  cup chopped cooked potato, carrot, turnip and/or rutabaga; cooked corn
    or cooked peas
¼  cup chopped onion
1  tablespoon steak sauce
   Milk
   Ketchup, gravy, pickles or dairy sour cream (optional)

**1.** Let piecrust stand at room temperature according to package directions. On a lightly floured surface, unroll piecrust and cut into four pieces. Roll each into a 6-inch circle.
**2.** For filling: In a small bowl, combine meat, potato, onion and steak sauce; toss lightly to coat.
**3.** For pasties: Spoon about ⅓ cup of the filling onto half of each piecrust circle. Lightly moisten edges with a little milk. Fold other half of piecrust over filling. Seal edges by crimping with tines of fork. Cut slits in the top of the pies to allow steam to escape. Brush with a little additional milk. Place pasties on an ungreased large baking sheet.
**4.** Bake in a 375° oven for 20 to 25 minutes or until piecrust is golden brown. Cool slightly on a wire rack.

Serve pasties warm with, if you like, ketchup, gravy, pickles or sour cream. **Makes 4 servings.**

TIP: When buying beef, veal, pork and lamb, the meat should have good color and appear moist but not wet. Any cut edges should be even, not ragged. When buying packaged meats, avoid those with tears or with liquid in the bottom of the tray. The meat should feel cold to the touch.

TIP: To protect the crimped edge from overbrowning, fold a 12-inch square of foil into quarters. Cut off 3½ inches from the folded corners; unfold. There will be a 7-inch hole in the center. Loosely mold foil over the edge of the pasties before baking.

## Yooper soul food

Pasty purists sometimes quibble: Is it PAST-ee or PAH-stee? Everyone agrees, it's never PASTE-ee. No matter how you say it, these hefty, hearty half-moon meat pies are the comfort food of the Upper Peninsula.

Pasties came to the region with 19th-century Cornish immigrants, who mined the UP's rich veins of copper. Miners' wives packed hot-from-the-oven pasties in lunch pails, and the pies were still warm when the lunch whistle blew. The pies soon caught on with miners of all ethnic backgrounds.

Almost every UP community claims a bakery or restaurant selling the signature pie, including Randall's in Wakefield *(above)*. Usually, the filling is a mix of ground beef, diced potatoes and/or rutabagas, onions and, sometimes, carrots. You can also order vegetarian pies.

## Appetizers

### TRIO MARGARITAS
*Red Mesa Grill, Boyne City*

>       Fresh Sour Mix (recipe follows)
>       Simple Syrup (recipe follows)
>       Salt or sugar
>       Lime wedges
>       Raging Rita Margarita:
> 3     tablespoons tequila
> 3     tablespoons Fresh Sour Mix
> 3     tablespoons orange juice
> 1     to 2 tablespoons Cointreau
>       Ice cubes
>       Missy Margarita:
> 6     tablespoons Fresh Sour Mix
> 3     tablespoons tequila
> 1     to 2 tablespoons Grand
>       Marnier
>       Ice cubes
>       Pineapple Margatini:
> ¼     cup Pineapple-Steeped Tequila
>       (recipe follows)
> 1     to 2 tablespoons Cointreau
> 2     tablespoons Fresh Sour Mix
>       Pineapple juice
>       Ice cubes

Prepare Fresh Sour Mix and Simple Syrup; set aside. To coat a glass rim, place salt or sugar in a shallow dish. Rub the rim of a margarita glass with a lime wedge. Invert glass and dip rim into salt or sugar. Shake off any excess; set glass aside.

**Makes 1 drink (each recipe).**

**For each Raging Rita Margarita:** Place 3 tablespoons tequila, 3 tablespoons Fresh Sour Mix, orange juice and 1 to 2 tablespoons Cointreau in a cocktail shaker with ice cubes. Cover and shake vigorously. Strain into salt-coated glass. Serve with lime wedge.

**For each Missy Margarita:** Place 6 tablespoons Fresh Sour Mix, 3 tablespoons tequila and the Grand Marnier in a cocktail shaker with ice cubes. Cover and shake vigorously. Strain into a salt-coated glass. Serve with lime wedge.

**For each Pineapple Margatini:** Place Pineapple-Steeped Tequila, 1 to 2 tablespoons Cointreau, 2 tablespoons Fresh Sour Mix and a splash of pineapple juice in a cocktail shaker with ice cubes. Cover and shake vigorously. Strain into a sugar-coated glass. Serve with a lime wedge.

Fresh Sour Mix: Stir together 1½ cups lime juice, 1 cup lemon juice and the Simple Syrup. Cover and chill up to 1 week. Makes about 2½ cups.

Simple Syrup: In a small saucepan, stir together ⅔ cup sugar and ⅔ cup water. Bring to boiling, stirring to dissolve sugar. Remove from heat and cool the syrup. Transfer to a small bowl; cover and chill. Makes about 1 cup.

Pineapple-Steeped Tequila: In a glass or ceramic bowl, stir together 2 cups tequila and ¼ cup packed brown sugar until dissolved. Stir in half a peeled, cored pineapple cut into chunks and half a split vanilla bean. Cover and chill for 1 week. Strain. Makes about 2 cups.

Continued from page 37

### WHITEFISH CAKES WITH PARSNIP FRITES
*Hanna Bistro, Traverse City*

**7.** In a very large nonstick skillet, heat the oil over medium-high heat until hot. Add four of the fish cakes. Cook, uncovered, for 5 to 6 minutes or until golden brown, turning once halfway through cooking. Transfer to a 15x10x1-inch baking pan. Repeat with the four remaining fish cakes.
**8.** Bake in a 375° oven about 10 minutes or until heated through.
**9.** Meanwhile, in a food processor or blender, puree roasted red sweet peppers. Set aside.
**10.** For each serving, spoon a mound of hot cooked brown rice in the center of a small plate. Place a fish cake on top of rice. Top with a handful of the

Parsnip Frites. Garnish plate with pureed roasted red peppers, basil leaves and additional parsley. **Makes 8 appetizer servings.**

Parsnip Frites: Peel 4 medium parsnips; cut crosswise into 3-inch pieces. Using a hand-held julienne slicer, slide parsnip pieces lengthwise over the stainless-steel blades to make ⅛-inch-thick strips. (Or cut each 3-inch piece lengthwise into quarters, then cut each quarter into ⅛-inch-thick strips.) Place parsnip strips in a large bowl of ice water; let soak for 10 minutes. Drain parsnips and thoroughly pat dry with paper towels.

In a 3-quart saucepan or an electric deep-fat fryer, heat 2 inches of vegetable or peanut oil to 375°. Fry parsnips, one-fourth at a time, about 1 minute or until crisp-tender and light brown. (Do not crowd. Be cautious of splattering oil. Maintain an oil temperature of about 350°.)

Remove parsnips from hot oil; drain on paper towels. Transfer parsnips to a wire rack set on a baking sheet, arranging them in a single layer. Keep warm in a 300° oven. Makes 2 cups.

## CHERRY BARBECUE WINGS
*City Park Grill, Petoskey*

- ½ of a 16-ounce package frozen, unsweetened pitted tart red cherries, thawed
- ½ cup ketchup
- 2 tablespoons packed brown sugar
- ½ teaspoon finely shredded lemon peel
- 1 tablespoon lemon juice

- 1 tablespoon cherry liqueur or cherry juice
- ½ teaspoon salt
- ½ teaspoon ground ginger
- ½ teaspoon liquid smoke
- ¼ teaspoon ground cinnamon
- ⅛ teaspoon ground allspice
- 2 pounds chicken wings (12)

**1.** For barbecue sauce: Drain thawed cherries, reserving 1 tablespoon of the cherry juice, if using instead of cherry liqueur. Place cherries in a blender or a food processor. Cover and blend or process until cherries are nearly smooth.

**2.** Transfer cherries to a medium heavy saucepan. Add ketchup, brown sugar, lemon peel, lemon juice, cherry liqueur or reserved cherry juice, salt, ginger, liquid smoke, cinnamon and allspice. Bring mixture to boiling; reduce heat. Simmer, uncovered, for 15 minutes, stirring occasionally.

**3.** Meanwhile, rinse chicken wings and pat dry with some paper towels. Cut off and discard tips of chicken wings. Cut wings at joints to form 24 pieces. Arrange the chicken wing pieces in a single layer in a 15x10x1-inch baking pan. Bake in a 375° oven for 30 minutes. Drain the fat from the wings. Return the chicken wing pieces to the baking pan.

**4.** Pour barbecue sauce over wings. Bake for 5 to 10 minutes more or until the chicken is tender and no longer pink. **Makes 10 appetizer servings.**

TIP: Discard used marinades. If you wish to use some of the marinade for basting, set aside a portion of it before adding it to poultry during cooking.

## RUSTIC POTATO SKINS WITH BASIL CREAM DIP
*Wickwood Inn, Saugatuck*

- 15 small round red potatoes (about 2 pounds)
- 1½ 8-ounce packages (12 ounces) cream cheese, softened
- 3 ounces Parmigiano-Reggiano or Grana Padano cheese, grated (¾ cup)
- ¾ cup shredded mozzarella cheese (3 ounces)
- ¼ cup mayonnaise
- ¼ cup pesto
- ¼ cup olive oil
- 1 tablespoon snipped fresh rosemary
- ½ teaspoon sea salt, kosher salt or ¼ teaspoon salt

**1.** Scrub potatoes thoroughly with a brush; pat dry. Prick potatoes with a fork; place on a large shallow baking pan. Bake, uncovered, in a 400° oven for 40 to 60 minutes or until tender. Remove pan from oven; cool. Reduce the oven temperature to 350°.

**2.** For dip: In a medium bowl, beat cream cheese, Parmigiano-Reggiano, mozzarella, mayonnaise and pesto with an electric mixer on low speed until combined. Evenly spread cheese mixture in a 9-inch pie plate. Bake, uncovered, in a 350° oven for 30 minutes or until bubbly.

**3.** For potato skins: When potatoes are cool enough to handle, use the tines of a fork and your thumbs to break each potato into 3 or 4 irregular (rustic looking) pieces. Use a teaspoon to carefully scoop out the inside of each potato piece, leaving a shell about ¼ inch thick. (Cover and chill leftover white portion for another use.) **4.** Place the potatoes, skin side down, in a single layer on a large shallow baking pan. Drizzle oil over potatoes; sprinkle with rosemary. Return to oven (time them to be finished with dip coming out of the oven) and bake for 20 to 25 minutes more or until crispy and heated through. **5.** To serve, place dip in a shallow bowl in the center of a serving platter. Surround with potato skins. Serve immediately. **Makes 8 to 10 servings.**

## Salads

### FRESH FRUIT SALAD WITH HONEY-RUM DRESSING
*Historic Holly Hotel, Holly*

- ¼ cup snipped fresh mint
- ¼ cup lime juice
- ¼ cup rum or orange juice
- ¼ cup honey
- 1 large cantaloupe or honeydew melon
- 1 16-ounce container

strawberries, hulled and halved or quartered
- 1½ cups green and/or red seedless grapes
- 4 kiwifruit and/or golden kiwifruit, peeled and cut into ½-inch pieces

**1.** For dressing: In a large bowl, whisk together mint, lime juice, rum and honey. Set aside.
**2.** Cut cantaloupe in half and remove the seeds. Use a melon baller to scoop out pulp. Add melon balls, strawberries, grapes and kiwifruit to dressing; toss lightly to coat. Let stand for 15 minutes to allow flavors to blend.

### CHERRY VINAIGRETTE
*North Peak Brewing Company, Traverse City*

- 1½ cups frozen unsweetened pitted tart red cherries
- ⅓ cup red wine vinegar
- ¼ cup dried cherries
- 3 tablespoons honey
- 1 large shallot, quartered
- 1 clove garlic, halved
- 1½ teaspoons Dijon-style mustard
- ¼ teaspoon dry mustard
- ⅛ teaspoon kosher salt or salt
- ⅛ teaspoon coarsely ground black pepper
- ¼ cup salad oil

**1.** In a small saucepan, heat frozen cherries, uncovered, over medium-low heat for 10 to 15 minutes or until cherries and their juices are reduced to ½ cup, stirring occasionally.
**2.** In a food processor or blender, combine cooked cherries, vinegar, dried cherries, honey, shallot, garlic, Dijon-style mustard, dry mustard, salt and pepper. Cover and process or blend until smooth. With the processor or blender running, add the oil in a thin, steady stream and process for 1 to 2 minutes or until the mixture thickens. Cover and chill for up to 1 week. Use as dressing over tossed salads.
**Makes about 1½ cups.**

### SPANISH GARLIC POTATO SALAD
*Zingerman's Delicatessen, Ann Arbor*

- 6 medium round red potatoes (about 2 pounds)
- 3 tablespoons sherry vinegar or white wine vinegar
- 1 teaspoon sea salt or kosher salt or ½ teaspoon salt
- ¼ teaspoon freshly ground black pepper
- 1¼ cups mayonnaise
- ⅓ cup snipped fresh Italian (flat-leaf) parsley
- 2 cloves garlic, minced
- 1 to 2 tablespoons milk (optional)

PHOTOGRAPHS, (FROM LEFT) MARK THOMAS, BOB STEFKO

**1.** In a large saucepan or 4-quart Dutch oven, place unpeeled potatoes and enough lightly salted water to cover. Bring to boiling; reduce heat. Simmer, covered, for 20 to 25 minutes or just until tender. Drain; cool slightly. Peel, halve and cut potatoes into ¼-inch slices.

**2.** In a large bowl, place potato slices. Sprinkle with vinegar, salt and pepper. In a small bowl, combine mayonnaise, parsley and garlic. Spoon over potatoes; toss lightly to coat. Cover and chill for 4 to 24 hours. Just before serving, if necessary, stir in 1 to 2 tablespoons milk to make creamy.
**Makes 6 to 8 servings.**

# Soups

### FISH CHOWDER
*Inspired by Michigan's Great Lakes Whitefish*

- 1   pound fresh or frozen skinless whitefish fillets, cod or haddock
- 2   large potatoes, cut into ½ inch cubes

- 1½  cups coarsely chopped carrots (3 medium)
- 1½  cups chopped celery with leaves (3 stalks)
- 1   cup chopped onion (1 large)
- 1   clove garlic, minced
- ½   teaspoon salt
- ½   teaspoon lemon-pepper seasoning
- 2   cups water
- 1   10-ounce can whole baby clams, rinsed and drained
- 1   cup half-and-half or light cream
- 1   cup milk
     Butter (optional)
     Freshly ground black pepper (optional)

**1.** Thaw fish, if frozen. In a 4-quart Dutch oven, combine potatoes, carrots, celery, onion, garlic, salt and lemon-pepper seasoning. Add the water. Bring to boiling, reduce heat. Simmer, covered, for 12 to 15 minutes or until potato is tender, stirring occasionally.
**2.** Meanwhile, rinse fish; pat dry. Cut fish into 1-inch pieces. Stir fish into vegetable mixture. Cook, covered, for 5 to 10 minutes more or until fish begins to flake when tested with a fork. Stir in clams, half-and-half and milk. Cook and stir until heated through.
**3.** Ladle soup into bowls. If desired, garnish each serving with a pat of butter and pepper. **Makes 6 servings.**

### CREAM OF REUBEN SOUP
*Stonehouse, Escanaba*

- 5   cups chicken stock or three 14-ounce cans reduced-sodium chicken broth

- 12  ounces cooked corned beef brisket, chopped, or 2½ cups chopped deli franks
- 1   8-ounce can sauerkraut, rinsed and drained
- ½   cup chopped onion
- 1 to 2 cloves garlic, minced
- ¾   teaspoon dried thyme, crushed
- ½   teaspoon dried tarragon, crushed
- ¼   teaspoon ground white pepper
- 1   bay leaf
- ⅓   cup cold water
- 3   tablespoons cornstarch
- 2   large carrots, coarsely shredded
- 12  ounces process Swiss cheese slices, cut up
- 1   cup shredded natural Swiss cheese (4 ounces)
- 1   cup whipping cream, half-and-half or light cream
     Rye Bread Croutons (see recipe, page 144)

**1.** In a 5- to 6-quart Dutch oven, combine chicken broth, beef brisket, sauerkraut, onion, garlic, thyme, tarragon, white pepper and bay leaf. Bring to boiling; reduce heat. Simmer, covered, for 30 minutes. Remove bay leaf; discard.
**2.** In a bowl, stir together the cold water and cornstarch. Stir cornstarch mixture and carrots into soup. Cook and stir until thickened and bubbly; cook and stir for 2 minutes more.
**3.** Reduce heat to low. Add the process and natural Swiss cheese; cook and stir until melted. Stir in whipping cream; heat through. Top each serving with some of the Rye Bread Croutons.
**Makes 8 servings.**

**Rye Bread Croutons:** Cut 4 slices rye bread into ½-inch pieces. Arrange pieces in a 15x10x1-inch baking pan. Bake in a 350° oven for 10 minutes or until bread pieces are dry and crisp, stirring once. Cool completely.

Continued from page 79

### THREE-ALARM LANSING FIRE CHILI
*Lansing Fire Department, Lansing*

**4.** In a skillet, cook the sausage over medium-high heat until no pink remains, using a wooden spoon to break up meat as it cooks. Drain fat. Cover and chill sausage until needed.
**5.** Add chocolate bar to tomato mixture, stirring until melted. Add shredded meat, sausage and corn. Simmer, covered, for 30 minutes more, stirring occasionally. Add the undrained chili beans. Simmer, covered, for 30 minutes more, stirring occasionally.
**6.** To serve, top chili with shredded cheese and, if you like, corn chips. **Makes 10 servings.**

# Main Dishes

### TARTARE OF AHI TUNA
*Saltwater at MGM Grand Detroit, Detroit. See photo page 8.*

 1  pound fresh sushi-grade Ahi tuna steaks
 4  medium fresh green and/or red jalapeño chile peppers, halved lengthwise
 ¼  cup sesame (not toasted) oil
 1  cup water
 1  tablespoon lemon juice
 1  small fresh pear
 4  cloves garlic, minced
 ½  cup pine nuts, toasted
 1  teaspoon sea salt or
    ½ teaspoon salt
 ½  teaspoon ground white pepper
 4  quail egg yolks (optional)
    Ground ancho chile pepper or chili powder
    Sliced fresh mint leaves
    Toast points

**1.** Using a very sharp knife, cut tuna across the grain into small cubes. Cover and chill until ready to serve.

**2.** For chile oil: Remove seeds and membranes from chile peppers; set aside. Finely chop chile peppers; set aside. In a small saucepan, heat sesame oil and the reserved seeds and membranes over low heat for 2 minutes or until heated through. Remove saucepan from heat. Let stand for 8 to 10 minutes or until desired temperature. Strain oil through a fine-mesh sieve; discard seed mixture. Cool chile oil to room temperature. Set aside.

**3.** In a small bowl, combine the water and lemon juice. Peel, core and finely chop pear. Add pear to lemon juice mixture; set aside. Just before serving, thoroughly drain pear.

**4.** For each serving, using a 2½-inch ring mold or round cutter, pack chilled tuna firmly and evenly into the mold. Unmold tuna into the center of a chilled dinner plate. If using quail egg yolk, make a small indentation in the top of the tuna mound (this gives the quail egg yolk a resting place). Surround tuna mound with about 2 tablespoons pear, ½ teaspoon garlic, 2 teaspoons jalapeño peppers and 2 tablespoons pine nuts. Sprinkle ¼ teaspoon salt and ⅛ teaspoon white pepper over tuna mound. If you like, place a quail egg yolk in indentation. Drizzle with 1 tablespoon of the chile oil. Sprinkle with ancho pepper and mint.

**5.** To eat, use a fork to thoroughly combine all of the ingredients. Serve with toast points. **Makes 4 servings.**
**CHEF TIP:** Because hot chile peppers contain volatile oils that can burn your skin and eyes, avoid direct contact with chiles as much as possible. When

PHOTOGRAPHS: (FROM LEFT) ROBERT JACOBS, KEVIN J. MIYAZAKI/REDUX working with chile peppers, wear plastic or rubber gloves. If your bare hands do touch the chile peppers, wash your hands and fingernails well with soap and water when you are done.

Continued from page 19

## COLOSSAL CRAB CAKES WITH SALSA
*Rattlesnake Club, Detroit*

**3.** For yellow salsa sauce: In a food processor or blender, combine the yellow and/or orange tomatoes, horseradish and half of the lime juice mixture. Cover and process or blend until smooth. Transfer to a small bowl; set aside.
**4.** For red salsa sauce: In a food processor or blender, combine the chopped red tomatoes, chipotle pepper sauce and the remaining lime juice mixture. Cover and process or blend until almost smooth. Transfer to another small bowl; set aside.
**5.** Bake in a 375° oven for 15 to 20 minutes or until heated through and golden brown. Remove from oven.
**6.** For each serving, place one-fourth

of the yellow salsa sauce on a plate. Top with a crab cake. Spoon one-fourth of the red salsa sauce over crab cake. Top with salad greens and garnish with tomatoes. **Makes 4 servings.**

## BARBECUED RIBS WITH CHERRY CHIPOTLE SAUCE
*Grand Traverse Resort & Spa, Acme*

- 1  tablespoon kosher salt
- 1  tablespoon garlic powder
- 1  tablespoon cumin seeds, toasted
- 1  tablespoon chili powder
- 1  tablespoon freshly ground black pepper
- 4  pounds pork loin back ribs (pork baby back ribs)
- 2  12-ounce cans beer or 3 cups apple juice
- ½  cup red wine vinegar
- ½  cup snipped fresh cilantro
     Cherry Chipotle Barbecue Sauce (recipe follows)

**1.** For dry rub: In a small bowl, combine salt, garlic powder, cumin seeds, chili powder and pepper. Trim fat from meat. Sprinkle mixture evenly over all sides of meat; rub in with your fingers. Place ribs, bone sides down, in a shallow roasting pan; cover pan with foil. Marinate in the refrigerator for 24 hours.
**2.** Uncover ribs. Add beer, vinegar and cilantro to roasting pan. Bake ribs, covered, in a 350° oven about 1 hour or until tender. Remove from pan and cool until ready to grill.
**3.** For a charcoal grill, arrange medium-hot coals around drip pan.

Test for medium heat above the drip pan. Place ribs, bone sides down, on grill rack directly over drip pan. Cover and grill about 30 minutes or until heated through and very tender, brushing with some of the Cherry Chipotle Barbecue Sauce during the last 10 minutes of grilling. (For a gas grill, preheat grill. Reduce heat to medium. Adjust for indirect grilling. Cover and grill as above.)
**4.** To serve, cut between bones to separate the ribs into serving-size portions of two or three ribs each. Reheat and pass remaining Cherry Chipotle Barbecue Sauce with the ribs.
**Makes 4 to 6 servings.**
Cherry Chipotle Barbecue Sauce: In a medium saucepan, combine 1 cup barbecue sauce, ¼ cup frozen cherry or cherry-apple juice concentrate and 1 to 3 canned chipotle peppers in adobo sauce, drained and chopped. Cook and stir just to boiling. Remove from heat. Brush sauce over ribs during the last 10 minutes of grilling. Makes about 1¼ cups.
Oven-Only Method: Cook ribs in oven as directed for 1½ hours. Brush ribs with Cherry Chipotle Barbecue Sauce the last 10 minutes of baking. Omit grilling step.
TIP: Grill Safety Precautions: Because grilling involves fire, it requires its own set of safety rules.
• Use charcoal or gas grills outside only—never in a garage, porch or enclosed area.
• Never leave a grill unattended or try to move it while it's in use or still hot.
• Allow coals to burn completely and ashes to cool for 24 hours before disposing of them.

## FESTOONED FETTUCCINE

*Herman's at Garland Lodge & Resort, Lewiston*

- 1 pound dried fettuccine
- 3 cups sliced fresh crimini or button mushrooms
- 1 cup finely chopped onion
- 6 large cloves garlic, minced
- 3 tablespoons olive oil
- 3 red sweet peppers, cut into thin strips (3 cups)
- 1 cup whipping cream
- ¾ cup crumbled Gorgonzola cheese (3 ounces)
- ⅓ cup snipped fresh chives
- 3 tablespoons snipped fresh parsley
- 3 tablespoons snipped fresh basil
- ¼ teaspoon salt

**1.** Cook the fettuccine according to the package directions. Remove from the heat. Drain and return to saucepan to keep warm.
**2.** For sauce: In a large skillet, cook mushrooms, onion and garlic in 2 tablespoons of the olive oil over medium-high heat for 4 to 5 minutes

or until vegetables are tender, stirring occasionally. Remove with a slotted spoon, reserving the oil in skillet.
**3.** Add the remaining 1 tablespoon olive oil to skillet. Add pepper strips to skillet. Cook about 5 minutes over medium heat or until tender; stir occasionally.
**4.** Add the whipping cream and cheese to the pepper strips in the skillet. Stir the mixture over medium heat until the cheese melts and the sauce thickens slightly. Stir in the mushroom mixture, chives, parsley, basil and salt.
**5.** To serve, pour sauce over the pasta and toss to coat. Transfer to a serving dish. **Makes 6 servings.**

## CHICKEN-SPINACH PITAS

*Sugar Bowl Restaurant, Gaylord*

- Nonstick cooking spray
- 1 cup sliced fresh mushrooms
- ½ cup chopped onion (1 medium)
- 6 cups torn fresh spinach (8 ounces)
- 1 tablespoon water
- 2 6-ounce packages boneless grilled chicken breast strips
- 1 cup shredded kasseri or mozzarella cheese (4 ounces)
- ¼ cup grated Parmesan cheese (1 ounce)
- ¼ cup bottled Caesar salad dressing
- 4 large pita bread rounds, halved and warmed

**1.** Lightly coat a large skillet with cooking spray; heat over medium heat. Add mushrooms and onion; cook for 5 minutes. Remove from heat.
**2.** Add spinach and the water to skillet. Cover and cook about

1 minute or just until spinach wilts. Stir in chicken; heat through. Add kasseri cheese, Parmesan cheese and Caesar salad dressing; toss gently to coat.
**3.** Serve chicken mixture in pita bread halves. **Makes 4 servings.**
**TIP:** To warm pitas, wrap in foil; heat in a 350° oven for 10 minutes.

## Side Dishes

Continued from page 17

## ROASTED GARLIC

*Bourbon Steak at MGM Grand Detroit, Detroit*

- 2 garlic bulbs
- 2 tablespoons olive oil
- Kosher salt or salt
- Freshly ground black pepper

**1.** Cut ½ inch off the tops of garlic bulbs to expose the ends of the individual cloves. Leaving garlic bulbs whole, remove any loose, papery outer layers. Place bulbs, cut ends up, on an 18-inch square double-

PHOTOGRAPHS: (FROM LEFT) KRITSADA; KEVIN I MIYAZAKI/REDUX

thickness of foil.

**2.** Drizzle bulbs with oil. Sprinkle with salt and pepper. Bring foil up around bulbs and fold edges together to loosely enclose.

**3.** Roast in a 400° oven about 25 minutes or until garlic feels soft when squeezed. Serve warm. (Or if you like, cool; squeeze bulbs from the bottoms and garlic will pop out of cloves.)

Continued from page 15

## ONION TARTS
*Rattlesnake Club, Detroit*

2   tablespoons olive oil
4   medium shallots, very thinly
      sliced
2   large cloves garlic, very thinly
      sliced
2   tablespoons olive oil
1   large sweet onion, such as
      Vidalia, Walla Walla or Maui,
      halved lengthwise and very
      thinly sliced
1   leek, trimmed, rinsed, well
      drained and white part only
      cut into thin strips
½   cup snipped fresh chives
½   cup grated Parmesan cheese

**1.** In a large nonstick skillet, heat the 2 tablespoons oil over medium heat. Add shallots and garlic. Cook about 8 minutes or until tender, stirring occasionally. Using a slotted spoon, transfer shallot mixture to a medium bowl.
**2.** In same skillet, heat the 2 tablespoons olive oil over medium-high heat. Add onion and leek. Cook about 10 minutes or until tender and golden brown. Add onion mixture to shallot mixture. Stir

Beef tenderloin steak on an onion tart and topped with a potato crisp, recipes below.

in chives and Parmesan cheese. Form onion mixture into four rounds, each about 3½ inches in diameter. Serve immediately or keep warm in a 300° oven for 20 minutes. Makes 4 tarts.

Continued from page 15

## POTATO CRISPS
*Rattlesnake Club , Detroit*

     Nonstick cooking spray
1   medium potato, cut lengthwise
      into ⅛-inch-thick slices
     Garlic salt, onion salt or salt

Lightly coat a baking sheet with cooking spray. Arrange potato slices in a single layer on prepared baking sheet. Lightly sprinkle with garlic salt. Bake in a 450° oven for 12 to 15 minutes or until crisp and golden brown. Transfer to a wire rack; cool for 10 minutes. Makes 4 servings.

Continued from page 25

## FRUIT SALSA
*Cygnus 27 at Amway Grand Plaza, Grand Rapids*

1   teaspoon grapeseed oil or
      olive oil
½   cup finely chopped onion
1   tablespoon grated fresh ginger
1   tablespoon finely chopped
      fresh lemongrass
1   fresh red Thai chile pepper,
      seeded and chopped
3   cups chopped fresh pineapple
1½  chopped fresh mango
     Kosher salt or salt
     Freshly ground black pepper

In a large skillet, heat oil over medium heat. Add onion, ginger, lemongrass and chile pepper. Cook about 5 minutes or until onion is tender, stirring often. Add pineapple and mango.

Cook for 5 minutes more. Season to taste with salt and black pepper. Serve warm. Makes 3½ cups.

**CHEF TIP:** Because hot chile peppers contain volatile oils that can burn your skin and eyes, avoid direct contact with them as much as possible. When working with chile peppers, wear plastic or rubber gloves. If your bare hands do touch the chile peppers, wash your hands and fingernails well with soap and water when you are done.

Continued from page 27

## PROVENÇAL VEGETABLE RATATOUILLE

*Amway Grand Plaza, Grand Rapids*

- 2 tablespoons olive oil
- ⅓ cup finely chopped red onion (1 small)
- 2 cloves garlic, minced
- 1 cup chopped zucchini (1 small)
- ½ cup chopped tomato (1 medium)
- 2 teaspoons snipped fresh basil
- ½ teaspoon kosher salt or salt
- ¼ teaspoon snipped fresh thyme
- ⅛ teaspoon ground black pepper

**1.** In a large saucepan, heat oil over medium heat. Add onion and garlic. Cook and stir about 2 minutes or until onion is tender.

**2.** Stir in zucchini. Cook and stir for 1 minute. Stir in tomato. Simmer, uncovered, about 2 minutes or until most of the liquid from the tomato is evaporated and the zucchini is tender.

**3.** Stir in basil, salt, thyme and pepper. Remove from heat; keep warm. Makes ¾ cup.

Continued from page 39

## LEMON ZABAGLIONE HOLLANDAISE SAUCE

*Trattoria Stella, Traverse City*

- 2 cups unsalted butter
- 4 egg yolks
- ¼ cup dry white wine
- 3 tablespoons lemon juice
- ½ teaspoon kosher salt or salt
- ½ teaspoon ground white pepper
- 1 to 2 tablespoons hot water

**1.** In a small saucepan, melt butter over low heat. Remove from heat. In the top of a double boiler, combine egg yolks, wine and lemon juice. Place over gently boiling water (top pan should not touch water). Cook, whisking rapidly, until egg mixture thickens and coats a metal spoon. Slowly drizzle melted butter into egg mixture while whisking constantly until thickened sauce drapes off spoon (should look like thin mayonnaise). Immediately remove from heat.

**2.** Stir in salt and white pepper. If sauce is too thick or curdles, whisk in the hot water. If you like, place sauce in a glass measuring cup and place measuring cup in a pan of gently simmering water to keep warm until ready to serve. Makes 3 cups.

Continued from page 77

## JASMINE RICE AND PAPAYA

*Tabor Hill Restaurant, Buchanan*

- ½ cup uncooked jasmine rice
- 1 tablespoon butter
- 1 tablespoon finely chopped green onion
- 2 cloves garlic, minced
- 1 teaspoon grated fresh ginger

1 cup water
¾ cup finely chopped papaya
  Kosher salt or salt
  Freshly ground black pepper

**1.** Rinse rice until water runs clear; drain well.
**2.** In a medium saucepan, melt butter over medium heat. Add green onion, garlic and ginger. Cook and stir for 2 minutes. Stir in drained rice. Cook for 2 minutes, stirring frequently. Carefully add the water. Bring to boiling; reduce heat. Simmer, covered, about 15 minutes or until rice is tender.
**3.** Remove from heat; stir in papaya. Let stand for 5 minutes before serving. Makes about 2½ cups.

## QUICK FIX CORN STICKS
*Bavarian Inn Restaurant, Frankenmuth*

1 cup cornmeal
¾ cup all-purpose flour
2 to 4 tablespoons sugar
2½ teaspoons baking powder
½ teaspoon salt
1 cup milk
2 eggs
¼ cup butter, melted

**1.** For corn sticks: Generously grease corn stick pans; heat prepared pans in a 400° oven for 3 minutes. For muffins: Grease twelve 2½-inch muffin cups or line with paper bake cups. Set aside.
**2.** In a medium bowl, stir together cornmeal, flour, sugar, baking powder and salt. In a small bowl, whisk together milk, eggs and melted butter. Add milk mixture all at once to cornmeal mixture. Stir just until moistened (batter should still be lumpy).
**3.** For corn sticks: Carefully fill preheated corn stick pans two-thirds full with batter. Bake in a 400° oven for 12 to 15 minutes or until edges are golden brown. (If you wish to make corn sticks with all the batter and have just one corn stick pan, bake several batches. The batter will hold while it waits to be baked.)
**4.** For muffins: Spoon batter into prepared muffin cups, filling cups two-thirds full. Bake in a 400° oven about 15 minutes or until edges are golden brown. **Makes about 20 corn sticks or 12 muffins.**

Continued from page 131

## TARTAR SAUCE
*Inspired by Michigan's Great Lakes Whitefish*

1 cup mayonnaise
2 tablespoons chopped sweet pickle
1 tablespoon finely chopped green onion
1 tablespoon snipped fresh Italian (flat-leaf) parsley
½ teaspoon finely shredded lemon peel
2 teaspoons lemon juice
1½ teaspoons snipped fresh dill
½ teaspoon paprika

In a bowl, combine mayonnaise, sweet pickle, green onion, parsley, lemon peel, lemon juice, dill and paprika. Makes 1¼ cups.

# Desserts

Continued from page 123

## CHERRY-BERRY PIE
*Jesperson's Restaurant, Petoskey*

**5.** If you like, brush the top piecrust with milk and sprinkle with additional sugar. To prevent overbrowning, cover the edge of the pie with foil.
**6.** Bake in a 375° oven for 30 minutes. Remove foil. Bake for 30 to 35 minutes more or until the filling is bubbly and piecrust is golden brown. Cool on a wire rack. If you like, serve warm with vanilla ice cream. **Makes 8 servings.**

Continued from page 45

## CHOCOLATE PASTRY TART SHELLS
*The Common Grill, Chelsea*

On a lightly floured surface, divide dough into four portions. Roll each dough portion from center to edge into a circle about 5 inches in diameter. Line four 4- to 4¼-inch tart pans that have removable bottoms with pastry circles. Press pastry into fluted sides of tart pans; trim edges.

Prick bottoms and sides of pastry shells. Line pastry shells with double-thick pieces of regular foil or single layers of heavy foil or parchment paper. If you like, fill with pie weights. Place tart pans on a large baking sheet.

Bake in a 350° oven for 15 minutes. Remove baking sheet from oven. Carefully remove the pie weights, if using, and the foil sheets. Return baking sheet to the oven. Bake for 5 to 8 minutes more or until pastry shells are firm and just beginning to brown around the edges. Remove from oven.

Brush bottoms of shells with 2 ounces melted bittersweet chocolate. Cool shells on a wire rack. Remove from pans. Makes four 4-inch shells.

Continued from page 45

## HOT FUDGE SAUCE
*The Common Grill, Chelsea*

- ⅓ cup semisweet chocolate pieces
- 2 tablespoons butter
- ⅓ cup sugar
- ⅓ cup whipping cream

Whipped cream and hot fudge *(below)* add to the decadence of the banana cream tart.

In a heavy small saucepan, combine chocolate pieces and butter; cook and stir over low heat until melted. Stir in sugar. Gradually stir in whipping cream. Bring to boiling; reduce heat. Boil gently for 5 minutes, stirring frequently. Remove from heat. Let stand for 10 minutes. Serve warm. Makes about ¾ cup.

Continued from page 45

## VANILLA BEAN WHIPPED CREAM
*The Common Grill, Chelsea*

- 1 cup whipping cream
- 2 tablespoons powdered sugar

Chill a medium bowl and beaters of an electric mixer. In the chilled bowl, combine whipping cream, powdered sugar and the reserved vanilla seeds (see Step 1 in Banana Cream Chocolate Tart, page 45). Beat with chilled beaters of an electric mixer on medium speed until soft peaks form (tips curl). Makes 2 cups.

Continued from page 115

## BUTTERDOUGH
*Dutch Delite Bakery, Holland*

- 1 cup cold butter
- 2 cups all-purpose flour
- ½ cup cold water

**1.** Coarsely chop cold butter. In a medium bowl, combine the butter, flour and the water. (Flour will not be completely moistened.)

**2.** Turn dough out onto a lightly floured surface. Knead dough by folding and gently pressing it for 10 to 12 stokes or until dough forms a rough ball (the dough will have some areas that look dry and some chunks of the butter will be visible).

**3.** Turn the dough out onto a well-floured surface. Roll dough into a 17x12-inch rectangle. Fold one-third of the dough over the center third and fold the remaining third over the top (creating three layers).

**4.** Cover the dough with waxed paper; chill for 5 minutes in the refrigerator.

**5.** Repeat rolling and folding into three layers. Cover; chill dough for 10 minutes. Repeat rolling and folding into three layers. Wrap the dough in plastic wrap; chill for 8 to 24 hours.

CHEF TIP: If edges crack while rolling, gently pinch the dough back together.

**Powdered Sugar Icing:** In a small bowl, combine 1 cup powdered sugar and 1 tablespoon milk. Stir in additional milk, 1 teaspoon at a time, until icing reaches glazing consistency. Makes ½ cup.

Continued from page 49

## ESTERHÁZY SCHNITTEN
*Hermann's European Cafe, Cadillac*

**5.** Bake in a 350° oven for 12 to 15 minutes or until cake springs back when lightly touched (center may dip slightly). Cool cake in pan on a wire rack for 10 minutes. Loosen cake from sides of pan by sliding a metal spatula between cake and pan. Invert onto a wire rack. Remove the pan; peel off the paper. Cool completely.

**6.** Cut the cake crosswise into four 10x3¾-inch strips.

**7.** To assemble, place one cake layer on a serving plate; spread with ¼ cup of the apricot preserves and one-third of the Vanilla Mousse. Top with a second cake layer; spread with ¼ cup apricot preserves and one-third of the Vanilla Mousse. Top with a third cake layer; spread with ¼ cup apricot preserves and the remaining Vanilla Mousse. Top with remaining cake layer.

**8.** For apricot glaze: In a small saucepan, melt the remaining ¼ cup apricot preserves and the water. Strain apricot mixture through a fine-mesh sieve. Brush apricot glaze in a thin layer over top of cake; let stand for 15 minutes. (If you like, cover and chill cake for up to 4 hours before applying Fondant Icing.)

**9.** In a small saucepan, cook and stir chocolate and shortening over low heat until melted. Transfer to a heavy resealable plastic bag; set aside. Pour warm Fondant Icing down the center of the cake. Using a thin icing spatula, work quickly to spread icing toward the edges (do not allow fondant to run down sides of cake).

**10.** Snip a small hole in one corner of the plastic bag with melted chocolate. Immediately squeeze chocolate in lengthwise stripes on top of the fondant icing. Using the tip of a knife

or the edge of the icing spatula, draw crosswise diagonal lines on top of the cake, alternating directions so the chocolate forms V shapes. Wipe blade with a damp cloth after each stroke. Let cake stand about 15 minutes or just until top is set. Cover loosely and chill cake for at least 2 hours or until ready to serve. For easier slicing, cut the cake while cold but let it come to room temperature before serving. If you like, serve with whipped cream.

**Makes 16 servings.**

**Vanilla Mousse:** In a small bowl, sprinkle 1¼ teaspoons unflavored gelatin over ¼ cup milk; let stand for 10 minutes. In a medium metal bowl or the top of a double boiler, beat 3 egg yolks and ¼ cup sugar with a wire whisk until combined. Place over gently boiling water (metal bowl or top pan should not touch water).

Cook, stirring rapidly with whisk, about 3 minutes or until egg mixture begins to thicken and coats a metal spoon (160°). Remove from heat.

Add gelatin mixture and 1½ teaspoons vanilla to warm egg mixture; whisk until combined. Beat with an electric mixer on medium speed about 5 minutes or until cool; set aside. Thoroughly wash beaters.

In a chilled small mixing bowl, beat ¾ cup whipping cream on medium speed until stiff peaks form (tips stand straight). Gently fold whipped cream, one-third at a time, into egg mixture. Cover and chill for at least 2 hours. Makes about 2 cups.

**Fondant Icing:** In a small saucepan, combine 1½ cups powdered sugar, 2 tablespoons water and 2 teaspoons light-color corn syrup. Cook, stirring constantly with a wooden spoon, over low heat for 2 to 3 minutes or until sugar dissolves. (Do not allow temperature of fondant to exceed 100°.) Remove from heat. Stir in ¼ teaspoon vanilla. (Mixture should be thin enough to pour, but thick enough to coat cake.) Use icing while warm. (If icing sets up before you finish, reheat over low heat.) Makes ½ cup.

## SPICED CHERRY PIE

*Inspired by Michigan's cherries.*
*See photo, page 92.*

- 5  cups frozen unsweetened pitted tart red cherries
     Cherry juice or water
- 1  15-ounce package rolled refrigerated unbaked piecrust (2 crusts)
- 1  cup sugar
- ¼  cup cornstarch
- 1  teaspoon ground cinnamon
- ¼  teaspoon salt
- ¼  teaspoon ground allspice or ground nutmeg
- 2  tablespoons butter
     Coarse sugar (optional)

**1.** Thaw frozen cherries in a colander over a medium bowl (2 hours), reserving juice. Measure drained juice and add enough cherry juice or water to measure ¾ cup.

**2.** Let piecrust stand at room temperature according to package directions. Unroll piecrusts. Ease one piecrust into a 9-inch pie plate, being careful not to stretch pastry. Do not prick pastry. Cut the remaining piecrust in ½-inch wide strips; set aside.

**3.** For cherry filling: In a medium saucepan, combine sugar, cornstarch, cinnamon, salt and allspice. Add the ¾ cup reserved juice and butter. Cook and stir over medium heat until thickened and bubbly. Remove from heat. Stir in the thawed cherries.

**4.** Pour the cherry filling into the pastry-lined pie plate. Weave strips over filling in a lattice pattern. Press strip ends into bottom pastry rim. Fold bottom pastry over strip ends; seal and crimp the edge of the piecrust. To prevent overbrowning, cover edge of pie with foil.

**5.** Place pie on the oven rack positioned over a baking sheet on the rack below. Bake in a 375° oven for 30 minutes. Remove foil. Bake for 30 to 35 minutes more or until filling is bubbly in the center and piecrust is golden. Cool on a wire rack for at least 2 hours before serving. To serve, sprinkle with some coarse sugar, if you like. **Makes 8 servings.**

TIP: Storing spices: Ground herbs and spices maintain good quality and aroma for 6 months. Store in a dry place away from sunlight and heat.

## MOM'S OATMEAL PIE

*Diana's Delights, Gaylord*

- 2  eggs, slightly beaten
- ¾  cup pure maple syrup
- ½  cup granulated sugar
- ½  cup packed brown sugar
- ½  cup milk
- ½  cup butter, melted
- 1  teaspoon vanilla
- 1  cup flaked coconut
- ¾  cup rolled oats
- ½  cup chopped walnuts
- 1  9-inch unbaked pastry shell
     Whipped cream (optional)

**1.** For filling: In a mixing bowl, combine eggs, maple syrup, granulated sugar, brown sugar, milk, butter and vanilla. Stir until well-combined.

**2.** Stir in the coconut, oats and nuts. Pour filling into unbaked pastry shell.

**3.** Bake in a 375° oven for 35 to 40 minutes or until a knife inserted near the center of pie comes out clean.

**4.** Cool on a wire rack. Chill in the refrigerator within 2 hours. Cover and chill for longer storage. If you like, serve pie with whipped cream. **Makes 8 servings.**

## CHOCOLATE-DRIED CHERRY CHEESECAKE
*The Cove, Leland*

    8 ounces unsweetened dark
        chocolate, chopped
 ⅓  cup butter
1½  cups purchased chocolate
        cookie crumbs
    6 ounces dried cherries (1¼
        cups), snipped
    3 8-ounce packages cream
        cheese, softened
1½  cups sugar
 ¼  cup Starbucks coffee liqueur,
        Kahlua, other coffee liqueur
        or strong coffee
    2 eggs
        Milk chocolate curls (optional)

**1.** Place chocolate in a heavy medium saucepan; stir over low heat just until melted. Remove from heat; set aside.
**2.** In a small saucepan, melt butter over medium heat. Add cookie crumbs; toss to mix well. Press crumb mixture onto the bottom and 1½ to 2 inches up the sides of a 9-inch springform pan. Wrap outside of the springform pan securely with heavy foil. Sprinkle dried cherries on the bottom crust; set aside.
**3.** In a large mixing bowl, beat the cream cheese with an electric mixer on medium-high speed for 3 minutes or until light and fluffy. Gradually beat in the sugar, ½ cup at a time, for 3 minutes or until mixture is completely smooth, scraping sides of bowl occasionally. Reduce speed to medium; beat in the melted chocolate until combined. Beat in coffee liqueur or coffee until smooth. Add eggs all at once; beat on low speed just until combined.
**4.** Pour filling into crust-lined pan. Place springform pan in a large roasting pan. (Make sure there is at least 1 inch between springform pan and edges of roasting pan.) Place roasting pan on oven rack. Carefully pour enough hot tap water into roasting pan to come halfway up sides of springform pan.
**5.** Bake in a 300° oven for 1¼ to 1½ hours or until edge of cheesecake is firm and center appears just set when lightly shaken. Carefully remove cheesecake pan from water bath; transfer to a wire rack and cool for 20 minutes. Remove foil. Loosen crust from sides of pan and cool for 30 minutes more. Remove sides of pan and cool completely. Cover cheesecake with plastic wrap and chill overnight. (Or store in refrigerator for up to 2 days.) To serve, cut into wedges and top with chocolate curls, if you like. **Makes 16 servings.**

**TIP:** For chocolate curls, draw a vegetable peeler across the narrow side of a chocolate bar (milk chocolate works best).

## LITTLE O'S
*Zingerman's Bakehouse, Ann Arbor*

    2 cups all-purpose flour
    1 teaspoon ground cinnamon
 ½  teaspoon baking soda
 ½  teaspoon fine sea salt or salt
 ⅛  teaspoon freshly grated
        nutmeg or ground nutmeg
    1 cup butter, softened
 ¾  cup packed brown sugar
 ½  cup pure maple syrup
    1 egg, lightly beaten
 ½  teaspoon vanilla
    2 cups organic rolled oats or
        quick-cooking rolled oats
    2 cups Red Flame raisins or
        raisins

**1.** In a bowl, combine flour, cinnamon, soda, salt and nutmeg; set aside.
**2.** In a large mixing bowl, beat butter with an electric mixer on medium to high speed for 30 seconds. Add brown sugar. Beat until combined, scraping sides of bowl occasionally. Gradually add maple syrup, about 1 tablespoon at a time. Beat in egg and vanilla until combined. Beat in as much of the flour mixture as you can with the mixer. Using a wooden spoon, stir in any remaining flour mixture. Stir in oats and raisins.
**3.** For each cookie, form 2 tablespoons of the dough into a ball. Place onto ungreased cookie sheets; press into ½-inch-thick rounds. Leave about 2 inches between rounds.
**4.** Bake in a 350° oven for 11 to 12 minutes or until lightly browned. Cool on cookie sheets for 1 minute. Remove to wire racks and let cool. **Makes about 30 cookies.**

# Location Index

# Recipe Index

PHOTOGRAPH: JOHN NOLTNER

## ACKNOWLEDGEMENTS

*Pure Michigan* is published by Meredith Corporation, publisher of *Midwest Living*® magazine.

BOOK EDITORS: Kristin Bienert, Editor, Custom Media and Barbara Morrow, Deputy Editor, Custom Media
BOOK DESIGN: Terri Ketcham, Associate Art Director and Geri Wolfe Boesen, Creative Director
PHOTO EDITOR: Joan Lynch Luckett, Editorial Project Manager

*Midwest Living* Editor-in-Chief: Greg Philby. Executive Editor: Trevor Meers. Travel Editor:
Kendra L. Williams. Assistant Travel Editor: Hannah Agran. Senior Food Editor: Diana McMillen.
Copy Chief: Maria Duryée

Director of Custom Publishing: Jodie Schafer. Contributors: Sandra Granseth, George Hendrix, Sandra Neff,
Dan Johnson and Katherine Rupp